W9-BBV-978

Osama BIN LADEN

Biography

BIN LADEN
Osama

Alex Woolf

Lerner Publications Company
Minneapolis

This book is dedicated to my brother Carl

A&E and **BIOGRAPHY** are trademarks of A&E Television Networks, registered in the United States and other countries. All rights reserved.

Some of the people profiled in this series have also been featured in the acclaimed BIOGRAPHY® series, on A&E Network, which is available on videocassette from A&E Home Video.

Copyright © 2004 by Lerner Publications Company

All rights reserved. International copyright secured. No part of this book may be reproduced, stored in a retrieval system, or transmitted in any form or by any means—electronic, mechanical, photocopying, recording, or otherwise—without the prior written permission of Lerner Publications Company, except for the inclusion of brief quotations in an acknowledged review.

This book is available in two editions:
Library binding by Lerner Publications Company,
 a division of Lerner Publishing Group
Soft cover by First Avenue Editions,
 an imprint of Lerner Publishing Group
241 First Avenue North
Minneapolis, MN 55401 U.S.A.

Website address: www.lernerbooks.com

Library of Congress Cataloging-in-Publication Data

Woolf, Alex.
    Osama bin Laden / by Alex Woolf.
       p.   cm. – (A&E biography)
    Summary: Presents biographical information about militant Islamic leader Osama bin Laden, including his role in international terrorism and the beliefs that fuel his actions.
    Includes bibliographical references and index.
    ISBN: 0–8225–5003–2 (lib. bdg. : alk. paper)
    ISBN: 0–8225–9900–7 (pbk. : alk. paper)
    1. Bin Laden, Osama, 1957– 2. Terrorists—Saudi Arabia—Biography—Juvenile literature. [1. Bin Laden, Osama, 1957– 2. Terrorists.]
    I. Title.
    HV6430.B55 W665 2004
    958.104'6'092—dc21   2002013958

Manufactured in the United States of America
1 2 3 4 5 6 – JR – 09 08 07 06 05 04

CONTENTS

Osama bin Laden is the founder and leader of the
international terrorist organization al-Qaeda.

Chapter **ONE**

SEPTEMBER 11, 2001

ON SEPTEMBER 10, 2001, OSAMA BIN LADEN, the Saudi-born terrorist and sworn enemy of the United States, visited the city of Qandahar in southern Afghanistan. Here he met with the country's leader, Mullah Mohammed Omar. The two men spoke quietly for half an hour inside a building enclosed by a high wall. As the meeting ended, the pair embraced each other warmly. It was a gesture of friendship and of farewell.

Around lunchtime the same day, bin Laden was driven by car to a whitewashed villa just outside Qandahar, where his four wives and many of his seventeen children were living. He gathered his family around him and explained to them that something big was about to happen and that they would not be able to see him for a while. They would be moved to a safer place later that day and then broken into smaller groups and taken secretly into neighboring Pakistan. Afghanistan, bin Laden was sure, would soon become a war zone. He himself was heading for a more remote location, as the Americans were certain to come looking for him.

Having said good-bye to his family, bin Laden had a few short meetings with senior officials of al-Qaeda, the terrorist organization he had created. Then he left Qandahar. Accompanying him in the small convoy of four-wheel-drive cars was a select group of close aides and armed fighters. They were heading for the Hindu Kush Mountains, a six-hundred-mile mountain range running from Pakistan to eastern Afghanistan.

By sundown they were high in the mountains. Waiting for them there were other al-Qaeda men, who had constructed a makeshift camp. After a few hours of sleep, the party set off once more, just before dawn, this time on horseback. It was an uncomfortable ride, especially for bin Laden, who suffered from back pain.

Late on the afternoon of September 11, they finally reached the remote cave that was their destination. From the outside, it looked like any other cave, but the narrow passage that led from the entrance soon opened into a larger area. The cave was outfitted with an array of technical equipment, including satellite television and access to the Internet, and domestic areas for eating and sleeping. While the other men in the party settled in, bin Laden watched CNN on the television and checked online news sites. It was 4:45 P.M. in Afghanistan, and 8:15 A.M. in the eastern United States. By this time, the biggest terrorist operation in history— planned by al-Qaeda and authorized by bin Laden himself—was under way. The four targeted aircraft had taken off. He waited tensely for the story to break.

American Airlines Flight 11 had taken off from Boston's Logan International Airport at 7:59 A.M., bound for Los Angeles, with ninety-two people on board. At 8:28 A.M., after the flight had been in the air for twenty-nine minutes, five passengers in business class stood up and forced their way into the cockpit, brandishing knives and box cutters. Soon afterward, a voice came over the intercom. "Nobody move, please. We are going back to the airport. Don't try and make any stupid moves." The pilot deliberately left his radio microphone open, so that air-traffic controllers on the ground could hear what was happening in the cockpit. However, the transponder, which allows controllers to identify the plane, had been switched off by one of the hijackers.

The hijackers killed the pilot and took control of the aircraft. The plane made an unexpected sharp turn to the left, setting it on a course headed for New York City. At 8:45 A.M., traveling at a speed of four hundred miles per hour, Flight 11 struck the World Trade Center near the ninety-first floor of the North Tower. The plane's

The World Trade Center in New York City, shown soon after the second plane had crashed into the South Tower on September 11, 2001

thousands of gallons of fuel ignited an immense orange ball of flame that billowed out from near the top of the skyscraper. Everyone on board the plane was killed instantly. Office workers on or around the ninety-first floor were also among the immediate victims. Moments later, CNN interrupted its programming to bring live coverage of the terrible event.

At first, people thought that the crash had been an appalling accident. Only bin Laden and his companions, watching the coverage from their remote mountain cave on the other side of the world, knew the truth. Already triumphant at witnessing this unprecedented strike against one of America's greatest landmarks, bin Laden continued to watch, knowing there was more to come. Eighteen minutes later, millions of people around the world watched in shock and disbelief as cameras recorded a second aircraft crashing into the South Tower of the World Trade Center. The awful truth then dawned that this wasn't an accident but a coordinated attack.

President George W. Bush, on a visit to Florida, told his audience that the country had suffered an "apparent terrorist attack." New York City authorities decided to close all the city's airports, bridges, and tunnels. At about 9:40 A.M., another aircraft flew in low over Washington, D.C., picked up speed, and plunged into the side of the Pentagon—the headquarters of the U.S. Defense Department. CNN broke into its coverage of the World Trade Center to show footage of the Pentagon.

Black smoke poured from one of the building's sides.

Minutes later, the Federal Aviation Administration announced that it was closing all the country's airports, stopping all domestic flights and outbound international flights, and diverting all inbound international flights to Canada. Bin Laden watched these developments with mounting elation, satisfied that he had succeeded in closing down air traffic throughout the entire United States.

Meanwhile, a fourth hijacked aircraft was still in the sky above Pennsylvania, possibly heading for a target in Washington, D.C., such as the Capitol or the White House. By this time, news of the other disasters had reached the passengers via their cell phones. Realizing that they were heading for their deaths anyway, some of the passengers decided to take matters into their own hands. After making final farewell phone calls to their loved ones, a group of them stormed the cockpit. Shortly afterward, the aircraft crashed into a wooded area eighty miles southeast of Pittsburgh. Everyone on board died instantly. The brave actions of those who confronted the hijackers probably saved the lives of many people on the ground.

Not yet aware of this failure, bin Laden witnessed the South Tower of the World Trade Center collapse in a gray avalanche of steel and rubble at about 10:00 A.M. Just before 10:30 A.M., the North Tower also fell.

Bin Laden, safe in his remote mountain hideaway, basked in the pleasure of seeing his despised enemy, the

President Bush speaks to his National Security Council team in the Cabinet Room of the White House shortly after the September 11, 2001, attacks.

United States, reeling at this series of devastating blows to symbols of its economic and military might. This attack was the culmination of a decade of bitter hatred. Close to three thousand people were killed in the attacks, making them the largest terrorist strikes ever to take place on U.S. soil. It had taken years of patient planning and millions of dollars of investment to bring his plan to fruition. With the September 11 attacks, the world would know what Osama bin Laden and his al-Qaeda network were capable of.

The city of Jidda in the 1930s as it would have looked to the young Mohammed bin Laden, Osama bin Laden's father

Chapter **TWO**

EARLY YEARS

OSAMA'S FATHER, MOHAMMED BIN LADEN, WAS born in the province of Hadramawt in Yemen, a nation on the southern tip of the Arabian Peninsula. Mohammed's father was a struggling farmer and beekeeper. He wanted a better life for his son. In 1930 Awad managed to secure Mohammed a job as a porter on the bustling dockside of Jidda in Saudi Arabia. Jidda was a rapidly expanding city in those days, full of opportunities for a bright, ambitious young man.

Before long, Mohammed managed, with the help of some contacts and the money he had saved as a porter, to start a small construction business. The profits from his first contracts were reinvested to buy newer, better equipment. By 1935 Mohammed was employing hundreds of workers with projects in towns and cities across Saudi Arabia. By the 1940s, he was a multi-millionaire with contacts among the al-Sauds, the Saudi royal family. His biggest breakthrough, which would elevate him into the elite of Saudi society, was obtaining the commission to build a palace for the future King Saud in 1948.

Mohammed's rise was meteoric, yet success never seemed to go to his head. Despite his great wealth, he remained a man of self-discipline, arriving at his office no later than 8 A.M. each day. He was also a committed Muslim, a follower of the religion of Islam. He prayed five times a day and made the hajj—a pilgrimage to the Islamic holy city of Mecca, Saudi Arabia—at least once a year. Mohammed was known for his generosity, donating large amounts to charity and sponsoring schools in Jidda for children of poor families. He renovated buildings in the holy cities of Mecca and Medina and rebuilt an important mosque in Jerusalem. These works won the bin Laden family the respect of many in Saudi Arabia, from the common people to the royal family.

Like most rich Muslim men, Mohammed wanted a large family and, starting in the 1940s, he began marrying a new wife every few years. Islam permits a man to have up to four wives at any one time. Mohammed kept three permanent wives, and others he would marry and then divorce, although they and their children would usually remain part of his household. In all, Mohammed married eleven women and had fifty-four children. One of them, born on March 10, 1957, was named Osama.

SON OF THE SLAVE

Osama was Mohammed bin Laden's seventeenth son. Osama's mother, Hamida, was the daughter of a Syrian family with whom Mohammed had business dealings. Mohammed met her on a trip to Damascus, Syria, and was struck by her beauty. Hamida was twenty-two years old when they married, and she had a lively, outgoing personality. Saudi Arabian society had stricter conventions than she had been used to in Syria. For example, women had to wear a burqa, a garment that

Muslim women wearing the burqa

covers their faces and bodies. The sheltered and disciplined life in Mohammed's household came as a shock to Hamida, and her cosmopolitan ways aroused the scorn of the other wives. Although Hamida was beautiful, Mohammed soon tired of her independent nature. By the time Osama was born, Hamida and Mohammed were already growing apart.

Once Hamida had fallen out of favor with Mohammed, the other wives were quick to reject her from their circle. They nicknamed her al-Abeda, meaning "the slave." Her status as an outcast was extended to her son, and he became the victim of cruel taunts by his half-siblings, who soon nicknamed him Ibn al-Abeda, "son of the slave." Isolation and rejection from the greater part of his family colored the earliest experiences of the young Osama, who grew into a shy and introverted boy.

Mohammed kept many homes in different parts of Saudi Arabia for his ex-wives, and Hamida was sent to live in the distant northern town of Tabuk. While still a young boy, Osama remained in the family home in Jidda, and he rarely saw his mother. The only close family attachment he formed was to Mohammed's first wife, al-Khalifa. She loved all of Mohammed's children as if they were her own, and the whole family regarded her as a mother figure.

One of the few highlights of Osama's lonely childhood was the twice-yearly family trip into the desert. Mohammed saw these outings as opportunities to build

Camel trains like this one have traveled through Saudi Arabia's desert for centuries. Osama rode camels in the desert with Prince Fahd and his sons.

the character of his sons, perhaps recalling his own modest roots and wanting to give them a taste of a tougher kind of existence. In the desert, it was very hot during the day and could be freezing at night. Frequent sandstorms filled the air with stinging grains of sand. Water, which was on tap at the bin Laden palace, had to be fetched from a well. Most of the bin Laden sons went on the trips only because their father had willed it, and they secretly missed the luxuries of the palace. However, Osama was the exception. Tall for his age, with a strong, lean physique, he loved the desert and spent his days there riding horses and camels and playing in the dunes. The desert excursions also gave Osama the chance to prove himself to Mohammed.

On one trip into the desert, when Osama was about nine, the bin Ladens were joined by Prince Fahd. Fahd, a friend of Mohammed's, was a member of the al-Sauds. Fahd brought some of his sons, who soon befriended Osama. They rode camels together and hunted for lizards, snakes, and other desert wildlife. Osama was happy to meet boys his own age who knew nothing of his problems at home. He began a lasting friendship with one of them, believed to be Abdul Aziz. On one occasion, the boys returned to camp with a full-grown dhub, a lizard that can grow to be as long as four feet. They are not aggressive creatures, but when provoked, they can bite. Causing panic among the rest of the camp, Osama and his friends brought the dhub to Mohammed and Prince Fahd. The two men were highly amused. But this humorous incident was a rare instance of contact between Osama and Mohammed. As much as Osama enjoyed these desert trips, they were too brief and infrequent for a strong bond to be forged with his father.

SCHOOL

Like his siblings, Osama was educated both at home and at al-Thagh, an exclusive private school near the palace. A whole wing of the palace was converted into a school, and the children were divided into classes according to their ages and abilities. Mohammed, having never had the benefit of formal schooling

Muslim children reading the Quran (the holy book of Islam). Osama and his siblings all had a solid grounding in Islamic scripture.

himself, made sure that his children were well educated, and he hired several highly qualified private tutors to guide the bin Laden children through their studies.

Mohammed was equally determined to give his children a thorough understanding of Islam. Islamic religious leaders and scholars were hired to teach at the palace. Mohammed also liked to surround himself with his children and talk about religion. He himself had enjoyed a successful life following the teachings and traditions of Islam, as laid down in the Quran, and he wished his children to do the same. He believed that their faith would help them deal with the pressures and temptations of the great wealth that they would all one day inherit.

Osama was a moderate student. He usually found a seat near the back of the class, and he only spoke when he was asked a question. An English teacher at al-Thagh named Brian Fyfield-Shayler recalled later that Osama "was very courteous—more so than any of the others in the class. Physically he was outstanding because he was taller, more handsome and fairer than most of the other boys . . . he was very neat, very precise and very conscientious. He wasn't pushy at all. Many students wanted to show you how clever they were. But if he knew the answer to something he wouldn't parade the fact. He would only reveal it if you asked him."

The only subject in which Osama really seemed to

ISLAM

slam was founded in the A.D. 600s by Muhammad, a respected and successful trader living on the Arabian Peninsula. Muslims believe that Muhammad was the last in a line of prophets including Moses and Jesus, and that his message came straight from God (Allah in Arabic, the historic language of Islam).

Muslims also believe that Allah passed on his message to Muhammad in the words of the Quran, the holy scripture of Islam. The Quran contains teachings about God, justice, and daily life, as well as Islamic versions of stories from the Bible.

Because it is regarded as the sacred word of Allah, the Quran is never translated, and Muslims all over the world learn to read and recite it in the original Arabic. Another source of guidance for Muslims is the Hadith, a collection of stories about Muhammad's own life.

Islam consists of six main beliefs, known as the Six Articles of Faith: belief in God, in the Quran, in the angels, in Prophet Muhammad and the prophets sent before him, in Judgment Day, and in Allah's power over human destiny. Muslims express their faith in actions, known as the Five Pillars of Islam.

shine was Islamic studies. In these classes, he was not at all reserved and was always the first to answer questions and take part in readings from the Quran. He did not simply learn chunks of the holy scripture but also liked to comment on them and try to interpret what he read. His evident enthusiasm for Islamic

These actions are:

- The Declaration of Faith (Shahadah) that there is no god but Allah, and that Muhammad is his prophet.
- Prayer (Salah) five times a day.
- Fasting (Sawm) during Ramadan and other holy times.
- Giving Alms (Zakat), donations to the poor.
- Pilgrimage to Mecca (Hajj) at least once in a lifetime, for those who are able.

Islam is a total way of life, influencing how believers eat, dress, and behave. For example, strictly devout Muslims are only supposed to eat meat slaughtered in a certain way. They should not drink alcohol or gamble, and they should dress modestly. These rules are expressed in Sharia (Islamic law). In countries with Islamic governments, such as Saudi Arabia, Sharia is enshrined in the nation's laws. For Muslims living in non-Islamic countries, it is more of a personal code.

A mosque, above, is the Islamic place of public worship.

thinking and discussion gave great pleasure to his father and helped to bring them closer.

A TRAGIC DEATH

In 1968 Mohammed bin Laden was returning from a business trip when his helicopter developed engine problems and crashed in the desert. He died instantly. His death caused great shock and distress at the family's palace, and it was soon filled with the sounds of mourning and children's sobs. Mohammed's body was retrieved and prepared that afternoon for burial. Soon after dawn the following day, his body, wrapped in a simple white cloth, was carried from the palace to the family plot in a nearby cemetery.

Mohammed bin Laden was greatly respected by the people of Jidda, and his death was a cause of great sadness in the city. Nearly ten thousand people lined the route to the cemetery. The Saudi king, Faisal, had been a close friend of Mohammed and was visibly upset. In a later television interview, Osama recalled the funeral, saying, "King Faisal cried. He said upon the death of my father that 'Today I have lost my right arm.'"

Osama, just ten years old at the time, was deeply scarred by the experience of losing his father, particularly after he had started to grow closer to him through their shared interest in Islam. Lacking a relationship with his mother and feeling little sense of kinship with his half-siblings, Osama had longed for the love and respect of his father. But his father was gone from his life. Osama grew even more introverted and withdrawn.

Immediately after the funeral, King Faisal met with the bin Laden family and told the children he was placing them under royal protection. Mohammed's estate was cared for by a royal committee, and the children would receive their shares of the inheritance when they were twenty-one years old. But the household could not continue as one unit without Mohammed at its head, and the wives, ex-wives, and children began to disperse to different parts of the kingdom.

Eventually Salem, the eldest son, took over the family business. Under Salem's direction, the business expanded into an international company. In addition to construction, the Bin Laden Construction Group became involved in oil exploration, mining, and telecommunications.

UNHAPPY YEARS

After the household broke up, Osama had been sent to live with his mother in Tabuk. She was pleased to see him, but Osama, still aching from the recent death of his father, was not ready to form a close attachment to a woman he hardly knew. He was polite to her, but his replies to her questions were brief and formal. He preferred to spend his time either in his room or exploring the monuments and mosques of Tabuk. After only two months, mother and son were barely speaking to each other. Osama, bored with Tabuk, wrote to his uncle Abdullah—Mohammed's brother, who was head of the family—and asked if he could return to Jidda. His request was granted.

Even back in Jidda, the following years were not happy ones for Osama. With the family dispersed, the palace was a lonely, empty place. Occasionally, Osama joined his family on trips to cities in the Arab world. He found himself particularly drawn to the famous mosques of Cairo, Egypt. But his relationships with his brothers and sisters did not greatly improve. Family members found Osama oversensitive, interpreting childish teasing as personal attacks.

According to some reports of his life, Osama's unhappy early teens were occasionally enlivened by trips to Europe with his family. Christina Akerblad, the owner of the Astoria Hotel in Falun, Sweden, recalls Osama visiting at the ages of thirteen and fourteen, the first time with a large number of his family, and the second time with just his older brother Salem. "I

The bin Ladens on vacation in Falun, Sweden, in 1971. Osama is second from the right, standing with his back against the car.

remember them as two beautiful boys," she said. "The girls in Falun were very fond of them. Osama played with my two young sons." Osama himself once told of a visit to London, England, where he stayed in fashionable Park Lane overlooking Hyde Park. He couldn't remember the name of the hotel, but he recalled "the trees of the park and the red buses."

At home, Osama continued his friendship with Abdul Aziz. Abdul lived at the al-Yamamah Royal Palace in Riyadh (the capital of Saudi Arabia), and the boys stayed in touch by phone and through letters. But their contact was sporadic. With the death of Mohammed, the link between the bin Ladens and the al-Sauds had weakened. Osama learned the hard way that he could no longer count on the privileged status he had once enjoyed. When he heard that Abdul Aziz was in Jidda with his father, Osama telephoned Prince Fahd's residence several times but received no reply. Finally he went to their home, but he was turned away. A little later, the royal family moved back to Riyadh. Osama never heard from Abdul Aziz again.

NEW EXPERIENCES

Beginning in about 1973, Osama made frequent trips to Beirut, Lebanon, which was well-known as a center of entertainment. At first he was shocked by the sight of Muslim women walking in public with their arms and legs uncovered. However, he quickly accepted the more relaxed attitudes of Lebanon, and he began to enjoy these visits as a release from the strict rules governing life in Saudi Arabia. He made new friends and went on swimming and boating trips. He also enjoyed frequent outings to movie theaters—a novelty for Osama, as such theaters were banned in Saudi Arabia.

For a rich Saudi boy from a sheltered background, the temptations of cosmopolitan Beirut were very great. At sixteen years old, he tried alcohol for the first time, and the following year he discovered Beirut's flashy nightclubs. He became a regular patron of these establishments, always arriving with a large crowd of friends, and he developed a taste for drinks such as whiskey and champagne. Inevitably his studies suffered, and although he remained courteous to classmates and teachers, he gave the impression that attending school was a little beneath him.

Osama's playboy lifestyle came to an abrupt end when civil war broke out in Lebanon in 1975 and Osama could no longer make trips to Beirut. Around this time, when he was seventeen, he got married. His wife, Najwa Ghanem, was a Syrian and a relative of his mother. She was just fourteen years old. Osama's

Destruction in the streets of Beirut, Lebanon, in the mid-1970s. The civil war there put an end to Osama bin Laden's visits to the city.

Pilgrims in Mecca gather at the Kaaba, the holiest structure in Islam, during the 1970s.

family, having heard reports of his wild behavior in Beirut, may have pressured him into this match in the hope that it might encourage him to be a more responsible person. And, outwardly, Osama showed every intention of changing for the better. At the urging of his elder brother Salem, he enrolled in a course in economics and management at King Abdul Aziz University in Jidda. Salem made sure that a key component of this course was civil engineering, so that Osama could later take up a useful role in the family business. Within a year, Osama and his wife had a son, whom they named Abdullah.

AWAKENINGS

During his mid-teens, bin Laden's early interest in Islam had declined. It had been replaced by the more immediate gratifications of easy friendships, alcohol, and fast cars. However, the experience of attending the university changed bin Laden profoundly. While there, he also took a course in Islamic studies. His teachers were Sayyid Qutb and Abdullah Azzam. Both of them were Islamic conservatives. They preached that the leaders of the Islamic world had been corrupted by too much contact with Western countries. They believed that Islamic countries needed to make a complete return to core Islamic values. Their message had a powerful effect on bin Laden. Azzam introduced bin Laden to the connected worlds of politics and religion. Azzam said that the Arab world required new political leadership if it was to restore the power of Islam. He advocated a jihad. The word *jihad* means "struggle" in Arabic. Azzam chose to interpret the word to mean a holy war against the infidels (referring to non-Muslims).

Under the influence of Azzam and Qutb, bin Laden began living in strict accordance with Islam. He prayed five times a day, gave up alcohol, and grew a long beard as a sign of piety. One of his brothers, Abdelaziz, remembers bin Laden "reading and praying all the time" during this period. Bin Laden also went to Mecca on the hajj around this same time.

ISLAMIC REVOLUTION

In February 1979, bin Laden watched with excitement as the Islamic conservative, Ayatollah Khomeini, took power in Iran. He found it inspiring to see an Islamic revolution in action. In November 1979, bin Laden was similarly impressed by the sight of Islamic radicals seizing the grand mosque in Mecca. In bin Laden's view, these events were practical examples of how actions could be used to advance Islam. Bin Laden yearned, too, for an opportunity to prove himself as a warrior for Islam. He got his chance in the last days of 1979, when the Communist Soviet Union invaded the Islamic country of Afghanistan. (Communism is a system in which control of wealth and property rests with the government. It does not support established religion, and many Communist governments do not allow people to practice their faiths.) For bin Laden and other devout Muslims, the invasion was the start of a holy war.

Osama bin Laden was happier living a rough existence in Pakistan than he had been surrounded by the luxuries of his family home in Saudi Arabia.

Chapter **THREE**

THE MILLIONAIRE MUJAHIDEEN

THE LEADERS OF THE SOVIET UNION CLAIMED THAT the occupation of Afghanistan was at the request of their fellow Communists in the People's Democratic Party of Afghanistan, who were at that time struggling to hold onto power in the country's capital city of Kabul. To the rest of the world, and to the independent-minded people of Afghanistan, it looked more like an aggressive act of conquest by a superpower against its much smaller neighbor. A fierce resistance to the occupation arose, and war ensued.

Soon after the invasion, the twenty-two-year-old bin Laden left his home in Saudi Arabia for Peshawar in northern Pakistan. Peshawar had become the center of Afghan resistance to the Soviet invasion. Bin Laden quickly saw that the resistance movement, known collectively as the mujahideen, was divided into several groups, each working independently and with little or no coordination. One leader whom bin Laden believed had potential to organize the groups was Abdul Rasul Sayyaf, a man bin Laden had previously met on the hajj. Sayyaf was setting up a propaganda campaign against the Soviets. After a month, bin Laden returned to Saudi Arabia and asked his brothers, other relatives, and friends at the university for funds to help Sayyaf's campaign. He raised a huge amount of money, some of

Armed mujahideen, left, formed a movement to resist the Soviet invasion of Afghanistan.

which was used to print and distribute anti-Soviet leaflets around Kabul. For the next two years, bin Laden traveled back to Saudi Arabia many times on fund-raising trips.

In February 1980, Sayyaf reintroduced bin Laden to his former university teacher, Abdullah Azzam, with whom bin Laden had lost touch since college. Azzam's ideas about jihad were inspiring Afghans and other Muslims, including many Arabs, in the fight against the Soviets. His motto was, "Jihad and the rifle alone: no negotiations, no conferences and no dialogues."

An immediate and powerful bond formed between the two men, greater than when bin Laden had been at the university. Bin Laden saw Azzam, then thirty-eight years old, as a spiritual and political guide, as well as the father figure he had been searching for ever since his real father died. Azzam, who had struggled to find a practical role for himself in the campaign against the Soviets, saw bin Laden as the ideal partner—young, full of enthusiasm for the cause, and with access to plentiful funds. Together they set up Maktab al-Khidamat (MAK), a support organization for Arabs and other Muslims who had come to join the struggle.

ORGANIZING THE RESISTANCE

Working as Azzam's deputy, bin Laden put his organizational abilities to use, quickly transforming a backroom office in Peshawar into the headquarters of MAK. With help from the Pakistani government, a

DR. ABDULLAH AZZAM

Dr. Abdullah Azzam, the man who would later become such an important influence on bin Laden, was born in 1941. As a boy, he joined the Muslim Brotherhood, a militant Islamic organization founded in Cairo in 1929. As he grew older, Azzam came to sympathize strongly with the Palestinians in the ongoing Palestinian-Israeli conflict, which had begun in 1948. He developed a hatred for Israel.

In 1966 Azzam obtained a degree in Sharia from Damascus University in Syria. Azzam was also a member of the Palestine Liberation Organization, a group dedicated to winning a homeland for the Palestinian people. The following year, Azzam moved to Jordan to take part in the Palestinian resistance. When the Palestine Liberation Organization was expelled from Jordan in 1970, Azzam went to Egypt, where he studied for his doctorate in Islamic law at al-Azhar University in Cairo. It was here that he met Sayyid Qutb, and together they developed the idea of a modern jihad. Azzam and Qutb's aim was to unite the whole Muslim world into a force to do battle with the enemies of Islam.

In the mid-1970s, Azzam was teaching Islamic law at the University of Jordan in Amman. Expelled for his extremist views, he moved to Saudi Arabia. After the Soviet invasion of Afghanistan, Azzam decided to devote his energies to the cause of the mujahideen.

reception center and training camps were established for newly arriving Arabs. Bin Laden began purchasing arms and equipment. He recruited experts in guerrilla warfare, a type of fighting used by small armed groups against more powerful enemies. Instead of confronting their enemy in open battle, guerrillas inflict damage by using other techniques, including ambush and sabotage. Bin Laden advertised MAK all over the Arab world. Within two years, MAK had recruited and trained approximately ten thousand volunteers who went on to fight in Afghanistan. MAK set up training camps for volunteers, where they were taught the techniques of guerrilla warfare and how to use weapons. The Arab volunteers became known as Arab Afghans.

MAK also attracted the attention of the American Central Intelligence Agency (CIA). The CIA was interested in helping the mujahideen fight the Soviet Union, which was also an enemy of the United States in the decades-long hostilities known as the Cold War. The CIA believed that MAK was worthy of support. Many millions of dollars of financial aid from the United States, as well as from bin Laden's own fund-raising efforts in Saudi Arabia, were distributed to the mujahideen by MAK.

Despite receiving American financial help, bin Laden had developed a hostile attitude toward the United States. In one early interview he said, "I always hated the Americans because they are against Muslims. . . .

Soviet tanks in Afghanistan during the 1980s. Soviet troops killed more than one million people during the war and forced about five million—one-third of the Afghan population—into exile.

We didn't want the U.S. support in Afghanistan, but we just happened to be fighting the same enemy."

At bin Laden's request, the bin Laden family made millions of dollars' worth of heavy construction machinery available to the mujahideen to help them create a defensive network for the Afghan resistance. Roads were cut through mountains, tunnels were built, and trenches were dug all along the Afghanistan-Pakistan border to create a permanent defensive base. Hospitals, arms dumps, training facilities, and accommodation for hundreds of fighters were constructed in giant cave complexes within the mountains of eastern Afghanistan. Bin Laden also used his own and his family's money to provide emergency aid, such as tents, blankets, and food for the many Afghan refugees fleeing across the border to Pakistan. The contributions of bin Laden and others like him were crucial.

The Soviet air force bombed Afghan towns and villages, while ground forces scattered land mines over inhabited areas and carried out large-scale attacks against civilians. The Arab volunteers whom bin Laden trained and sent into battle fought back fiercely, often desperately, alongside native Afghans. They were helped by the mountainous terrain of Afghanistan, which provided plenty of places for a smaller, weaker force to hide out and ambush a larger army.

During the early 1980s, bin Laden was content to keep a low profile, allowing Azzam to act as MAK's emir (leader). However, it was not long before bin Laden's behind-the-scenes activities began attracting attention. Western journalists in Pakistan heard stories of a "Saudi sheikh" (Arab leader) who visited wounded fighters in Peshawar hospitals, offering them cashew nuts and chocolates. The man would note down their names and addresses, and shortly afterward a generous check would arrive at their families' homes. This man may have been bin Laden—who could afford to be generous. He was by that time a rich man, having inherited millions of dollars from his share of his father's inheritance. Through careful investment, this money was earning him a substantial income.

However, bin Laden was not generous only with his money but also with his time. One former Afghan mujahideen told of how he once asked bin Laden for lessons in Arabic, so that he could read the Quran. According to this man, bin Laden spent many hours

Mujahideen receive training in weapon use and warfare. About twenty-five thousand Arabs traveled to Pakistan to join the Afghans in their struggle against the Soviets.

patiently teaching him. Other resistance fighters from this period say that bin Laden made cash donations toward marriages, shoes, and watches for their poor relatives. Bin Laden may have learned the value of acts of charity from his father, but these gifts and actions also served another purpose: they helped to build his reputation among young, impressionable recruits and to create a strong sense of loyalty toward him.

HOUSE OF THE FAITHFUL

Beginning in 1983, bin Laden and Azzam rented a house in a suburb of Peshawar called Hayatabad. The house also functioned as a reception center for the thousands of Arab volunteers arriving in the city. It was one of several large stone houses in a quiet street full of the colorful blossoms of flowering bougainvillaea. They called it Beit-al-Ansar, or "House of the Faithful." Neighboring houses were used as offices by other mujahideen groups, and by the mid-1980s the area had become a center for the Afghan resistance. Bin Laden received new arrivals at Beit-al-Ansar and then sent them on to the various fighting units in Afghanistan.

Conditions in Beit-al-Ansar were rudimentary. Despite his wealth and status, bin Laden slept on the floor with the other MAK officials, lying on thin pallets laid out in their offices. They debated Islam and Middle Eastern history long into the night. At this stage, bin Laden's radical views were only half-formed, but they were already heavily influenced by Azzam. Bin Laden had begun to be openly critical of the Saudi royal family, despite their generous donations to the Afghan campaign. He believed that their support for conservative Islam was not genuine but designed simply to help them hold onto power. Bin Laden's knowledge of history was hazy at best, but he liked to read about Islamic warriors of the past, perhaps seeing himself as their successor.

Bin Laden's generosity with his own money, his commitment to the struggle, and his willingness to live roughly despite his privileged background made him very popular among his fellow mujahideen. One of

Osama bin Laden, second from left, with his fellow mujahideen. Bin Laden was convinced of the spiritual importance of the Afghan conflict, viewing it as a way for Muslims to support Islamic governments and ideals.

them said, "He not only gave us his money, but he also gave himself. He came down from his palace to live with the Afghan peasants and the Arab fighters. He cooked with them, ate with them, dug trenches with them. This is bin Laden's way."

On the Front Line

Bin Laden spent most of the period between 1984 and 1986 in Pakistan, although he did make occasional trips to Saudi Arabia. Most of his time on these trips back home was spent fund-raising or briefing Saudi intelligence on the state of the Afghan campaign.

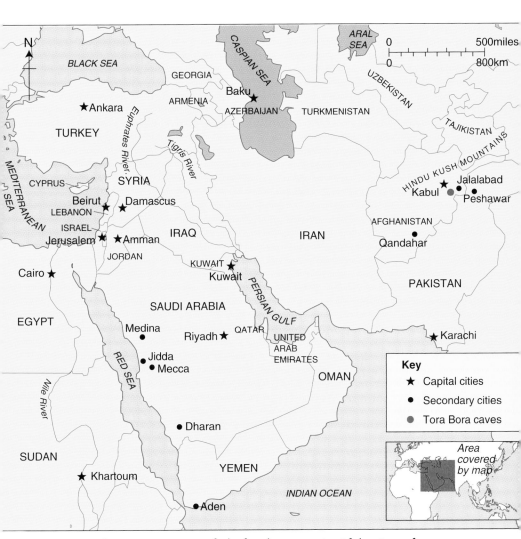

Arab recruits came to fight for the cause in Afghanistan from all over the Islamic world, but mostly from Saudi Arabia, Yemen, and North Africa.

Bin Laden's family saw little of him during his involvement in the Afghan war. His wife remained in Saudi Arabia, although his son Abdullah, who was twelve years old at the time, visited him once in Afghanistan in 1986.

By 1986 the war was in stalemate. Soviet forces had established control of the cities, while the mujahideen remained strong in the rural areas and the mountains. Both sides launched brief attacks into enemy territory, but no significant gains were being made. Bin Laden had grown frustrated with his role on the sidelines and decided it was time to see some real action. He took command of a group of Arab-Afghan fighters who had graduated from one of his MAK camps. Bin Laden and his men were involved in five major battles and hundreds of small operations and exchanges of fire.

Their first encounter with the enemy was during the successful defense of a mujahideen base in Afghanistan that was subjected to an assault by Soviet forces in April 1986. Later that year, bin Laden and fifty of his men stood their ground against a Soviet infantry and helicopter attack on a town called Jaji, near the border with Pakistan. Bin Laden's fighters managed to hold out for about one week before being forced to withdraw. The stand at Jaji against greatly superior forces was trumpeted as a victory in newspapers in the Arab world. A senior mujahideen commander, Mia Mohammed Aga, recalled, "[bin Laden] was right in the thick of it. I watched him with his . . . [rifle] in his hand under fire from mortars and the multiple-barrelled rocket launchers."

Bin Laden gained the respect of his men because of his bravery in battle, but also because he was prepared to live like them in caves and carry out basic duties. Bin Laden's exploits on the front line were reported by Arab journalists in Peshawar. The reports were widely published in Arabic-language newspapers, especially in Saudi Arabia, adding to his growing status as a war hero. Bin Laden's reputation inspired many others to try to emulate him, leading to a rush of new recruits to the MAK camps.

Bin Laden himself may have contributed to his own myth with some of his statements. "Once," he claimed, "I was only. . . [98 feet] from the Russians. They were trying to capture me. I was under bombardment but I was so peaceful in my heart that I fell asleep. This experience has been written about in Islam's earliest books. I saw a . . . mortar shell land in front of me, but it did not blow up. Four more bombs were dropped from a Russian plane on our headquarters, but they did not explode."

As bin Laden was gaining more of a following, he was also growing more intolerant of those who did not share his conservative religious views. One Afghan fighter reported that bin Laden had refused to speak to him during one battle because he was clean-shaven—a violation of traditional Islamic requirements. As the conflict wore on, bin Laden seemed to grow more

Soviet tanks and armored personnel carriers withdraw from Afghanistan in 1988.

fanatical, and he encouraged a similar fanaticism in his men. This mindset is illustrated by his own account of an episode during a battle when the mujahideen were besieging the eastern city of Jalalabad. "I took three Afghans and three Arabs and told them to hold a position," he said. "They fought all day, then when I went to relieve them in the evening the Arabs were crying because they wanted to be martyred. I told them that if they wanted to stay and fight they could. The next day they were killed."

VICTORY

By 1988 the Soviet Union was no longer able to sustain its mounting human and economic losses in the war, and the Soviet government announced its plan to withdraw from Afghanistan. In April of that year, a peace agreement was signed in Geneva, Switzerland, and the ten-year Afghan-Soviet War was over. Bin Laden was elated by this news. It was his view that the victory was entirely due to the actions of the mujahideen and the support that they had received from Arab and Islamic countries.

It would be a full year before the last Soviet troops departed, and fierce fighting continued against the government in Kabul. However, bin Laden's time as a mujahideen was drawing to a close. He began to consider what he should do next with his life.

At the end of the war in Afghanistan, bin Laden was determined to continue the fight against the enemies of Islam in other parts of the world.

Chapter **FOUR**

TERROR INCORPORATED

WHILE BIN LADEN WAS BUSY FIGHTING THE Soviet forces in Afghanistan, his friend Azzam was at work spreading his ideas about jihad among the mujahideen fighters on the Afghanistan-Pakistan border. Azzam was also developing his plans for the future. Azzam believed that when the war was over, the MAK organization should be put to a new purpose furthering the cause of Islamic revolution in other parts of the world. Many thousands of mujahideen, especially those from Arab countries, had been trained at MAK camps and retained bonds of loyalty to MAK. Azzam foresaw a future role for these mujahideen as a mobile force that could be deployed to fight in defense of Muslims wherever they were suffering oppression.

THE BIRTH OF AL-QAEDA

Toward the end of the war, when he was not on the front line, bin Laden spent his time at Beit-al-Ansar. The large stone house in Hayatabad had by this time been extended to include a number of outbuildings to make room for the ever-increasing numbers of newly arriving Arab recruits. The sheer number of MAK-trained volunteers who had passed through Beit-al-Ansar by 1988 was causing administrative problems. The paperwork recording the movements of volunteers from reception and training to their front-line postings had fallen behind. Bin Laden was concerned that he could not provide answers to inquiries from families about their loved ones. He therefore decided to create a new administrative department in order to track the movements of MAK-trained fighters. He based this department at Beit-al-Ansar, which he renamed al-Qaeda (the Base). Bin Laden took personal charge of al-Qaeda, though it remained part of the MAK organization. At al-Qaeda bin Laden compiled a vast database of mujahideen to keep track of their experience and personal information. Bin Laden also hoped to use this database to recruit fighters for future operations.

Beit-al-Ansar had been the reception center for many thousands of incoming Arab fighters during the course of the war. Toward the end of the conflict, as al-Qaeda, it played the same role in reverse. During 1988 and 1989, as the fighting began to wind down, Arab-Afghan fighters began coming down from the mountains. Usually their first stopping point on arrival in Pakistan was al-Qaeda. It was a place where friends were reunited and veterans would swap stories. The fighters felt euphoria at the victory but also sadness at its cost in the lives of comrades. A connection had grown between these men because of their shared experiences, and they wanted to keep in touch.

Many Arab veterans felt strong bonds of loyalty to bin Laden because of his generosity and his willingness to live and fight alongside them. They continued to believe—as he did—in the principles of Islamic fundamentalism that had originally brought them to Afghanistan. Their exposure to the ideas of Azzam and other Islamists encouraged them to continue the jihad in their home countries. Like bin Laden, they despised the Western-leaning governments of many of the nations in the Arab world. Bin Laden encouraged them to use the skills they had gained in the Afghan war to set up secret antigovernment groups. He promised them financial support and instructed them to contact him in Jidda, the city to which he planned to return eventually.

Although bin Laden and Azzam agreed on the principles of supporting Muslims in struggles around the world, they disagreed on tactics. One issue on which they differed was terrorism. Bin Laden supported the use of violence and terrorism to achieve political goals, but Azzam did not. When a group of Egyptian MAK veterans came to them with a request to set up a terrorist organization in Egypt, bin Laden was happy to give them his support. However, Azzam opposed the idea, believing that terrorism would never work against the Egyptian government. He also felt that terrorism went against Islamic law, because of the danger of killing innocent women and children.

Bin Laden had surpassed his mentor Azzam in his fanaticism. His experiences of fighting in the Afghan war had hardened him against violence. He had become convinced that Allah was on his side and that the deaths of innocent people were a necessary price in the ongoing battle against the enemies of Islam. Bin Laden had formed highly radical and aggressive views on how best to carry forward the jihad. His plan was to turn al-Qaeda into a worldwide terrorist force, with semi-independent cells (groups) in many different countries. He planned to use this force to help bring about the destruction of the United States and its allies. He also wished to establish a united Islamic world under one central leadership.

Bin Laden was no longer in awe of Azzam, and he found it increasingly difficult to accept him as leader of MAK. After moving for a brief time to Khost, Afghanistan, bin Laden returned to Hayatabad. He set up new guesthouses and training camps with the aim of establishing al-Qaeda as a separate organization from Azzam's MAK. When bin Laden tried to take over a MAK training camp called al-Masada on the

Afghanistan-Pakistan border and use it as al-Qaeda's headquarters, Azzam angrily refused to allow it.

The power struggle between the two men had reached a critical point. Aware that the older man was holding back his plans, bin Laden plotted to overthrow his former friend and install himself as leader of MAK and al-Qaeda. On November 24, 1989, while Azzam was driving to a Peshawar mosque for Friday prayers, a remote-controlled bomb blew up his car. Azzam was killed in the attack. Also killed in the blast were his two sons. The attack was carried out by the Egyptian terrorist group to which Azzam had refused to grant MAK funds. Bin Laden's involvement in the assassination has not been proven, but many observers believe that he was aware of the plans for it.

While alive, Azzam had been a restraining influence on bin Laden. He had encouraged bin Laden in the view that support should be built through inspirational speeches and persuasion, rather than random killing. With Azzam's death, bin Laden was free to pursue his plans to reshape al-Qaeda as an international terrorist force. Yet bin Laden was careful never to criticize Azzam publicly, and he always spoke of him admiringly as the founder and guiding force behind MAK and al-Qaeda.

HOMECOMING

Bin Laden returned home in the summer of 1989 to a hero's welcome. He was thirty-two years old. The Saudi press had reported his actions in Pakistan and Afghanistan to an admiring readership. For days after his return, his face appeared in all the newspapers, and for several months he could not go into a coffee shop in Jidda without being mobbed by autograph hunters. Projecting an unassuming image, he insisted that he wished only to lead a quiet life, working for the family business.

Bin Laden was happy to let people see him as a modest war hero. However, the truth was somewhat different. In 1980 bin Laden had departed for Afghanistan as an idealistic young man, eager to become a warrior for Islam. But his experiences there had changed him. In the intervening years, bin Laden had begun to view the al-Sauds with contempt. He believed that they had squandered the great wealth that Allah had given them through oil. He saw their Western lifestyle—their luxurious homes and foreign sports cars—as a betrayal of Islam. In one interview, he said, "Any government that sells its peoples' interests and

Bin Laden viewed shopping malls like this one in Riyadh, Saudi Arabia, and other symbols of the material values of the West with increasing contempt.

betrays its people and takes actions that remove it from the Muslim nation will not succeed. . . .We predict that . . . .they will disperse and disappear. After Allah gave them property on the most sacred land and gave them wealth that is unheard of before from oil, still they sinned and did not value Allah's gift."

While keeping up the appearance of a responsible executive working for the Bin Laden Construction Group, bin Laden used his office to maintain contacts with his former comrades from the Afghan war, in places such as Egypt, Yemen, and Algeria. Like him, they embraced a fundamentalist form of Islam and hated their Westernized leaders. He encouraged them in their anti-government activities and even sent financial support. Bin Laden himself began speaking out against the al-Sauds in the more conservative mosques in and around Jidda.

INVASION!

On August 2, 1990, Iraq, led by President Saddam Hussein, invaded the small nation of Kuwait. In neighboring Saudi Arabia, this news was greeted with great shock and alarm. Bin Laden, outraged and also excited by this turn of events, forgot his differences with the al-Sauds and immediately flew to King Fahd's palace in Riyadh. The king was too busy to see him, so he made an offer to Prince Sultan, who was both Fahd's brother and the minister of defense. Bin Laden told him he could raise a Muslim army through his contacts from the Afghan war. Within two days, he promised, he could provide thousands of armed and trained fighters to defend the Saudi border against Iraqi attack. Prince Sultan said he would put the offer to Fahd. Bin Laden began making preparations. For several days, he waited by his cell phone for a call from the palace. None came.

Then, on August 7, bin Laden learned that American troops were moving into Saudi Arabia to protect Saudi oil supplies. The Saudis were to join a U.S.-led coalition with the aim of liberating Kuwait, in a conflict that became known as the Gulf War. For bin Laden, this news was a cruel and hurtful blow. It confirmed all his worst fears about the Western-oriented attitudes of the Saudi monarchy. In the months that followed, he watched with an increasing sense of bitterness and humiliation as U.S. troops poured into his country. He saw the Americans as infidels trespassing on the holiest land of Arabia. Taking on the role that bin Laden felt should have belonged to his Islamic Saudi-Afghan army, the U.S. soldiers led the forces that ejected the Iraqis from Kuwait.

U.S. firefighters prepare to cap a burning Kuwaiti oil well—one of many fires set by retreating Iraqi troops at the end of the Gulf War.

The U.S. flag is raised at the American embassy in Kuwait following the victory against Iraq in the Gulf War.

TURNING POINT

The blow that fell on August 7, 1990, marked a turning point in bin Laden's life. From that day, the anger he felt toward the Saudi government and the United States swelled into an all-consuming hatred that would set him on an increasingly violent and deadly path.

In the aftermath of the Gulf War, bin Laden's rebellious attitude turned to open hostility. He spoke out against the Saudi government and the United States and went to mosques to circulate thousands of tapes expressing his views. He also began to raise an army.

Bin Laden's fury grew still further when American troops stayed on after the war, remaining at their long-established military bases in Saudi Arabia. Their presence appeared to him to be in defiance of the dying words of Prophet Muhammad: "Let there be no two religions in Arabia."

The al-Sauds did not approve of bin Laden's public condemnation of their policy to allow American bases in their country. They confiscated bin Laden's passport, and security forces began to harass him in the street. A relative recalled him returning home one day with a black eye and covered in blood. On another occasion, bin Laden's farm outside Jidda was raided by the Saudi National Guard. The authorities also placed financial pressure on the bin Laden family by threatening to cancel valuable government contracts unless Osama bin Laden ceased his political activities.

Bin Laden was determined to get out of Saudi Arabia. He spoke to his brother Bakr, explaining that he needed to visit Pakistan to finalize a valuable road-building contract that he had secured for the Bin Laden Construction Group. Bakr agreed to intercede with the government, and bin Laden's travel documents were granted. In April 1991, bin Laden flew to Karachi in Pakistan. He then wrote to Bakr, telling him he wasn't coming back and apologizing for betraying his trust.

Bin Laden knew that he was not much safer in Pakistan than he had been in Saudi Arabia. If requested to by the Saudis, Pakistani authorities would certainly arrest him and send him back home. Bin Laden did not waste any time. He flew straight to Peshawar, and from there to an Afghan al-Qaeda base in the mountains near Jalalabad. It felt good to be back in the Afghan mountains with his supporters, but bin Laden was disappointed by the state of the country's internal political affairs. The mujahideen had broken into factions that were fighting each other for control of Kabul and other cities. Meanwhile, many Afghans were starving. The war-torn, divided country could not provide a viable base for al-Qaeda.

The Saudi government had asked Pakistan for help in tracking down bin Laden. Pakistan's secret service had orders to arrest bin Laden, so he looked for a place to relocate. One country that welcomed him was Sudan in northern Africa. The leader of Sudan's ruling National Islamic Front, Dr. Hassan al-Turabi, was a great admirer of bin Laden and shared his vision of Islam. He was happy to offer him refuge and a new base for al-Qaeda. Bin Laden accepted the offer and flew to Sudan in December 1991.

SUDAN

Within a few weeks of his arrival, bin Laden had rented a suite of nine offices in Sudan's capital, Khartoum, and he began the difficult process of relocating al-Qaeda. He would play a double role in Sudan, working both as a businessman and as a terrorist.

As a businessman, bin Laden established a new construction business called al-Hijrah. With the help of al-Turabi, the business secured several large-scale contracts, including the development of a new airport at Port Sudan on the Red Sea and a four-lane, 745-mile highway linking Khartoum with Port Sudan. These projects were followed by contracts to improve the country's railway system and to build a huge dam. Within a few months, al-Hijrah was making millions of dollars in profit. Bin Laden went on to establish several

DR. HASSAN AL-TURABI

Dr. Hassan al-Turabi is an Islamic scholar who was educated at the Sorbonne in Paris, France, and at the University of London. Those who know him say he is an intelligent, charming man. An expert in Islamic law, with a deep knowledge of the Quran, he is also very good at communicating with and relating to Western audiences.

Al-Turabi became a leader of the Sudanese Muslim Brotherhood in the early 1960s, but his faction of the Brotherhood was dissolved by the Sudanese government in 1969. Eight years later, he was appointed attorney general of Sudan and presided over the establishment of Sharia in Sudan. Under his application of this system of law, harsh punishments, such as stoning, amputation, flogging, and hanging, were imposed for offenses such as theft and adultery.

Sudan's government was overthrown in 1985, and al-Turabi formed an extremist Islamic party called the National Islamic Front. In June 1989, Omar Hassan al-Bashir took power in Sudan in a military coup. Al-Bashir was a devout Muslim, and during his rule

more successful enterprises in fields as diverse as import-export, mineral and oil extraction, currency trading, genetic research, and farming. Bin Laden's business empire soon extended beyond Sudan to encompass interests all over the Arab world, as well as in Europe, China, Malaysia, and the Philippines.

Bin Laden was fortunate to have found a new source

Al-Turabi aimed to create a pure Islamic state. He welcomed the presence of al-Qaeda in Sudan. In return, bin Laden invested millions of dollars in the Sudanese economy.

he was strongly influenced by al-Turabi. Al-Turabi, as the effective ruler, began to lead Sudan down an extremist path. He offered Sudan as a base for Islamic fundamentalist groups, who paid the Sudanese government in return for a place from which to operate. This system opened the way for Sudan to become a major sponsor of world terrorism. Under al-Turabi, Sudan also became a police state (a country in which the government uses secret police to exercise repressive control). Many human rights abuses were committed, including torture, imprisonment and execution without trial, and the denial of freedoms of speech, assembly, and religion.

of income. Because he had left Saudi Arabia in such haste and secrecy, he had been unable to withdraw much of his personal fortune before his departure. Furthermore, those funds that he did manage to take with him were rapidly being drained by the costs of running al-Qaeda camps and by his financial support for Islamic groups in various countries in the region.

Bin Laden was happy to leave most of his business affairs to managers, while he devoted his time to his real interest: al-Qaeda. He believed that the only way to build a united Islamic world was through force. His aim was to overthrow the corrupt governments of the Islamic states and to remove the taint of Western influence. Eventually, he hoped, national boundaries could be removed to create one mighty Islamic empire powerful enough to challenge the Western world.

To achieve any of this, bin Laden needed help. He established links with about twenty groups involved in terrorism and guerrilla warfare in Egypt, Iran, Sudan, Yemen, Saudi Arabia, and Somalia. While he agreed with the aims of these groups, he found their vision limited in scope and their organization poor. They tended to focus only on struggles within their own countries, without seeing the fight in the context of a global jihad. They acted independently of each other, without coordinating their activities, and they did little strategic or long-term planning. In bin Laden's view, al-Qaeda could help them in these areas. It could play a valuable role as a multinational support group, financing and orchestrating the activities of Islamic militants worldwide. Bin Laden's vision could be described as "Terror Incorporated:" a global business to export terrorism around the world.

Al-Qaeda provided large sums of money to Islamic groups in Jordan and in Eritrea, a nation to the east of Sudan. The group also sent money to Baku, the capital of Azerbaijan, to help smuggle Islamic soldiers into nearby Chechnya, a Muslim-populated region fighting for its independence from Russia. Al-Qaeda also donated men, arms, and money to support Bosnian Muslims in a war with Serbia. Bin Laden's organization may have trained the Somalis who attacked American forces in Mogadishu, Somalia, in 1993. Bin Laden later spoke proudly of al-Qaeda's role in the killing of American soldiers in Somalia. However, it is unlikely that his fighters were directly involved in the battle.

During most of his time in Sudan, bin Laden lived and worked in a three-story al-Qaeda guesthouse in a rich suburb of Khartoum. His life there was simple and

A U.S. marine warns reporters to keep back during the 1993 fighting in Mogadishu, Somalia.

down-to-earth. Just as he had at Beit-al-Ansar, bin Laden mixed freely with his followers and bodyguards, praying and eating with them, and happily discussing Islam and the jihad. In his spare time, he enjoyed riding horses and attending horse races with al-Turabi's son Isam. One Saudi businessman who visited bin Laden during this period commented, "When I observed his house and his way of living, I couldn't believe my eyes. He had no fridge at home, no air conditioning, no fancy car, nothing."

Bin Laden also owned a small farm on the banks of the Blue Nile. He spent his weekends there, riding horses. His followers swam and played soccer. However, bin Laden never joined them in these sports. Aside from riding, his only other leisure activity was reading books on Islamic thought and current affairs.

Chairman of the Board

Al-Qaeda was run much like a large corporation. Bin Laden acted as chairman, with a board of directors known as the *shura majlis*. The shura majlis was made up of many of bin Laden's trusted followers from the Afghan war. Below this board, the organization was split into several departments that were responsible for terrorist activities, finance, payroll, human resources, travel, religious matters, and media relations. Al-Qaeda even had an in-house interpreter of dreams: a man called Abu al-Hasan al-Masri. According to one former member of al-Qaeda, "If anyone had a dream and believed that his dream could come true, he would go and tell [al-Masri] . . . . He's a scholar for that."

As he had done with the mujahideen in Afghanistan, bin Laden kept files on all of his staff members in Sudan, including their family details, aliases, and previous record of employment. He studied these files before entrusting anyone with a new task. He liked to involve himself in the recruitment and promotion of staff, but once people were in position he generally left them to do their jobs. He was never known to get angry with employees. When one staff member stole the equivalent of several thousand dollars, bin Laden asked only that he pay the money back. To dismiss the employee might have caused him to retaliate, which would pose a threat to the organization's security.

Bin Laden's office was plain. Its whitewashed walls were decorated only with framed posters of famous mosques and quotes from the Quran. Bin Laden worked at a very ordinary, inexpensive chipboard desk, and he used an old-fashioned dial telephone and cheap pens. He did not even have very much security until attempts were made to assassinate him. After that, security was tightened, and any visitors to his office were first searched by armed militiamen.

On an average morning, bin Laden would hold meetings with his directors and staff members, both collectively and individually, and take telephone calls. Sometimes he and his staff discussed new ideas and proposals from other terrorist groups. Bin Laden liked

Bin Laden is often seen in peaceful-looking poses like this one. His mild appearance gives no clue to his militant nature.

these discussions to be open. He valued the approval of ordinary Muslims, and even junior members of his staff were encouraged to offer their suggestions for future targets for terrorist attack. However, once the decision was made to move ahead with an operation, the planning was done in private by bin Laden and senior al-Qaeda directors. For security reasons, these planning meetings sometimes took place in the middle of a field at one of bin Laden's farms outside Khartoum.

By the time bin Laden was running al-Qaeda from Sudan, he had acquired a confidence that he had lacked as a shy and gangly youth. At six feet five inches tall, he easily dominated meetings, despite his soft voice and gentle, courteous manner. Something of his youthful shyness remained, however, and it took him time to feel at ease with new acquaintances. He liked to reflect for a while before speaking on any subject, and even then he generally spoke little, preferring to listen to those around him. He liked meetings to be informal and tried to put his visitors at ease. He sat with them on cushions arranged in a circle on the floor, and tea or Turkish coffee was often served. Those who have met bin Laden vary in their impressions of him. Some have found him charming company, while others have found something sinister about this quiet, polite man who is capable, with a whispered instruction, of setting in motion a terrorist attack anywhere on the globe.

ON THE ATTACK

By 1993 al-Qaeda was the world's biggest terrorist organization, and bin Laden had become one of the most powerful men in the global Islamic fundamentalist movement. That year al-Qaeda expanded its operations to strike the United States directly. In February 1993, a van carrying a bomb parked in the basement of the World Trade Center in New York City. When the bomb detonated, the explosion left a crater 150 feet in diameter and more than five stories deep. The attack killed six people and wounded more than one thousand. Ramzi Yousef, a senior field operative for al-Qaeda, was widely believed to have masterminded the bombing. Although the twin towers of the Trade Center did not collapse as they were intended to, bin Laden praised Yousef afterward, saying, "I remember him as a Muslim who defended Islam from American aggression. . . . America will see many youths who will follow Ramzi Yousef." But bin Laden did not reveal Yousef's connection to al-Qaeda, and the terrorist group never claimed responsibility for the attack. In the words of one operative, "Everyone knows that we were behind it and responsible for that action. Why claim credit and become identified and then hunted down?"

Aware of bin Laden's ongoing involvement in terrorism, the Saudi government tried hard to stop him from continuing these activities. In part, they were concerned that he might direct attacks at their kingdom. At least three delegations were sent to Sudan to ask bin Laden not to target Saudi Arabia. Bin Laden later said, "[the Saudis] sent my mother, my uncle, and my brothers in almost nine visits to Khartoum asking me to stop and return to Arabia to apologize to King Fahd. . . . I refused to go back."

The Saudi government tried other methods of putting pressure on bin Laden. In 1994 they revoked his citizenship and froze his assets inside the kingdom. Strong evidence suggests that they tried to assassinate him. In February 1994, a gunman opened fire on bin Laden's home in Khartoum. Bin Laden was not there, and the attacker was shot and wounded by police. Not long afterward, bin Laden's son Abdullah was attacked in Khartoum's central market. These incidents were dramatic warnings to bin Laden of the dangers facing him and his family. After this realization, he scaled down his social activities, such as attending horse races, and strengthened his personal security staff.

Suspecting Saudi involvement in the assassination attempts, bin Laden launched an intense campaign against the al-Sauds, supplying arms, explosives, and extra manpower to anti-government cells within the

Hosni Mubarak, president of Egypt, survived an assassination attempt by al-Qaeda in 1995.

kingdom. Al-Qaeda operatives planted several large car bombs in Riyadh in 1995. These bombings were aimed at American targets as part of bin Laden's campaign to rid Saudi Arabia of its American presence.

Al-Qaeda's activities also continued elsewhere. In February 1995, one plot was foiled when Ramzi Yousef was arrested in Pakistan. Yousef had been working in the Philippines, planning future attacks that included the hijacking and destruction of eleven U.S. aircraft. In June an al-Qaeda team attacked the motorcade of Egyptian president Mubarak on an official visit to Ethiopia. Mubarak escaped unharmed, and a later investigation traced the attack's roots to Sudan and al-Qaeda. Egypt, Britain, and the United States demanded that bin Laden be expelled from Sudan. When the Sudanese government refused, the United States increased its military assistance to Sudan's hostile neighbors, Uganda, Eritrea, and Ethiopia.

Ultimately, Sudan's President al-Bashir and Hassan al-Turabi bowed to international pressure. In March 1996, al-Turabi visited bin Laden at his offices and told him that Sudan could no longer host al-Qaeda. But bin Laden was already planning a return to Afghanistan.

Taliban militia burn films in front of a movie theater in central Kabul, Afghanistan. In addition to banning movies, Taliban leaders also prohibited television, music, and soccer.

Chapter FIVE

THE TALIBAN

AT ABOUT THIS TIME, BIN LADEN HEARD OF A radical Islamic student movement called the Taliban that was seeking power in Afghanistan. Impressed by their strict Islamic ideals, he agreed to help fund their campaign.

By the time bin Laden returned to Afghanistan in May 1996, the Taliban had taken control of Kabul and most of the rest of the country. Bin Laden was given a warm welcome by the Taliban leader, Mullah Mohammed Omar, who received him like family. Bin Laden pledged formal allegiance to Omar, the man Taliban members called *emir al-momineen*—"leader of the faithful." The personal bond between the two men was cemented by a formal alliance between the Taliban and al-Qaeda. The terrorist group formed guerrilla units to help the Taliban in their fight against the rebel United National and Islamic Front for the Salvation of Afghanistan (UNIFSA), also known as the Northern Alliance. The Northern Alliance was composed of many different groups that had joined forces to try to win power in Afghanistan. They included the fighters of former mujahideen leader Ahmad Shah Massoud, as well as a militia led by Abdul Rashid Dostam, a former army general.

In return for al-Qaeda's support, the Taliban regime offered them weapons, equipment, training facilities, and a secure base of operations. During the first year back in Afghanistan, bin Laden stayed in Jalalabad, overseeing the transfer of al-Qaeda to its new base and recruiting more followers. He lived in a newly built house at Hadda Farm, an agricultural area near Jalalabad. Bin Laden led a simple life, without any luxury. After dawn prayers, he studied the Quran for several hours. Breakfast consisted of dates, yogurt, flat Afghan bread, and black tea. Lunch and dinner were similarly plain.

Bin Laden preferred not to meet visiting journalists at Hadda but in caves in the nearby mountains. One journalist who interviewed him described the visit, saying, "It was not comfortable. His quarters were built in an amateurish way with the branches of trees. He had hundreds of books, mostly theological treatises. . . . I found him to be sincere. . . . His followers, really,

really believe in him. They can see this millionaire, who sacrificed all those millions, and he is sitting with them in a cave, sharing their dinner, in a very, very humble way."

Image was important to bin Laden, and he controlled how he was portrayed to ordinary Muslims. Several widely distributed posters, approved by bin Laden, showed him riding a white horse. This was supposed to identify him in people's minds with the prophet Muhammad, who also fought on a white horse. Similarly, he often liked to be pictured wearing the Palestinian kaffiyeh, or headdress, to show solidarity with the Palestinian struggle for statehood. Another favored head covering was a plain white turban common to Muslim religious figures. He wore this to give people an impression of his status as an Islamic leader, though in reality he had had no religious training beyond his boyhood schooling. The Arabian knife he often wore at his belt—a weapon commonly worn by Arab leaders—was supposed to show his legitimacy as a ruler. The ring he wore when making important declarations had a black stone set in silver, symbolizing Mecca, to remind his audience of his intention to free Saudi Arabia of the Americans and their supporters, the al-Sauds.

As al-Qaeda's new base took shape, the group's assets were slowly transferred to Jalalabad. While bin Laden's legitimate businesses remained in Sudan, their profits continued to provide the funds for his true interests.

THE TALIBAN

The Taliban was a student movement that emerged in Afghanistan during the civil war that followed the Soviet withdrawal in 1991. The movement was led by the conservative Islamic cleric Mullah Mohammed Omar. Born around 1960 near Qandahar, Mullah Omar was educated in Pakistan. He studied religion until joining the mujahideen, and he lost an eye in battle during the war with the Soviet Union.

Mullah Omar grew disillusioned with the mujahideen after the Soviet defeat, when the rebel forces quickly split into rival factions that began to jostle for power. He was also upset by the breakdown of law and order in Afghanistan. The departing Soviet forces left huge stocks of weapons, which fell into the hands of different warrior factions, leading to years of civil war. He recruited students from Islamic schools to form a new movement preaching a return to a purer form of Islam. Known as the Taliban, the movement spread quickly through Afghanistan, attracting many former mujahideen with the clarity and force of its message. Armed Taliban fighters captured the southern city of Qandahar in November 1994. This victory was the beginning of a series of successes that culminated in the taking of Kabul in September 1996—a brutal operation in which Taliban members tortured and killed former Afghan prime minister Najibullah and his brother, displaying their bodies and labeling them as enemies of Islam.

After September the Taliban was seemingly unstoppable, as more people flocked to what looked like a winning cause. The opposition fighters of the Northern Alliance were pushed back into a small area in the north of the country, and the Taliban announced itself as the new government. Ordinary Afghans welcomed the new leadership as a force for stability after many years of warfare and turmoil.

However, the Taliban's policies went much further than simply imposing law and order on the country and stamping out corruption. Mullah Omar and his followers aimed to create their vision of the world's purest Islamic state. They set about banning all influences that they viewed as corrupting, such as television, music, and movies. Women faced very extreme restrictions. They were denied education and the right to work, and they were forced to cover themselves from head to foot in the burqa. They were not allowed to leave their homes unless accompanied by a male relative.

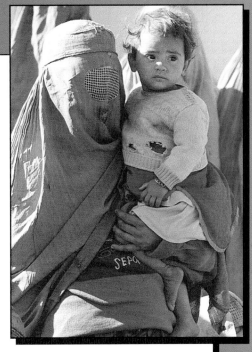

An Afghan woman, wearing a full burqa, carries her child through the streets of Kabul.

Adultery was punishable for both men and women by one hundred lashes or stoning to death. The hands and feet of thieves were cut off, and those who did not pray five times a day or fast in the daylight hours during the Islamic holy month of Ramadan were sent to prison.

After bin Laden was suspected of planning several terrorist attacks, the Taliban found itself under increasing international pressure to hand him over to face charges of terrorism. Taliban leaders refused. The United Nations imposed economic sanctions on Afghanistan, and when most foreign aid workers were withdrawn following several kidnappings, conditions rapidly declined. People all over the country suffered from acute poverty and starvation. Many were forced to eat leaves and grass, and some people sold their children to survive.

Afghan farmers raise poppy plants, from which heroin is manufactured.

And, through the Taliban's aid, al-Qaeda also had a new source of funds: drugs.

By 1996 Afghanistan's economy was in shambles. But the country was still one of the world's leading producers of opium poppies, from which narcotic drugs such as heroin can be made. Opium was the country's only significant export, and the Taliban was involved in encouraging, protecting, and taxing the industry. While there is no evidence that bin Laden and al-Qaeda were directly involved in the drug trade, they almost certainly benefited from the wealth that the industry brought to the Taliban. And, although strict Islamic law forbids Muslims to use drugs, bin Laden justified this deadly industry by saying, "The West is exporting to us its corrosive culture. We are exporting something back that corrodes their society."

Meanwhile, bin Laden continued with his plan to

A terrorist bombing destroyed U.S. military housing near Dhahran, Saudi Arabia, in 1996.

unify Islam into one powerful force by negotiating an alliance with Iranian-backed terrorist groups such as Hezbollah. This was a delicate task because bin Laden was a Sunni Muslim, and Iranians followed the Shiite branch of Islam with significantly different traditions. Nevertheless, the groups agreed to form a new organization, to be called Hezbollah International. This merger dramatically increased the range and power of Islamic militancy. In June 1996, Hezbollah International struck its first blow, detonating a massive truck bomb at the U.S. military housing complex of Khobar Towers near Dhahran, Saudi Arabia. The explosion killed nineteen U.S. service people and wounded more than four hundred. While the Saudi government blamed Iranian terrorists for the attack, they also suspected that bin Laden had been involved.

Going Underground

During the early 1990s, despite bin Laden's growing status as the world's leading terrorist, his family had not given up all hope of bringing him back into the fold. Some of them felt that it might still be possible for him to change his ways. Several of his brothers and cousins, as well as his uncle Abdullah, had visited him in Khartoum. Whenever a member of his family arrived, bin Laden welcomed them with great warmth and plied them with questions about their lives back home. However, when the subject moved on to bin Laden's activities, he forcefully defended himself and rejected any notion of changing his ways or returning to Saudi Arabia. Occasionally, bin Laden himself called family members, sometimes late at night, simply to swap gossip or to reminisce.

After the Khobar Towers operation, however, all of this changed. The bin Laden family was horrified to hear about bin Laden's suspected involvement in this attack. They had always made clear their support for the al-Sauds and their hatred of terrorism. From this point on, the family cut off contact with bin Laden. As far as the bin Ladens were concerned, Osama bin Laden was no longer part of the family.

Bin Laden also knew that the Khobar Towers

bombing had made him a target for the CIA and the Saudi secret service, and he lowered his public profile. He could no longer hold general meetings in his office or appear in public, as he had in Sudan. He changed his living arrangements, moving between several remote houses in the Jalalabad area, where his wife and children stayed, and a few camps in the mountains.

Bin Laden no longer used a satellite phone for communicating, concerned that the CIA might use its signals to track him. Instead, he dictated messages to an aide who then made the telephone call from a different location. He rarely remained in the same place for longer than two nights. When he traveled, he did so anonymously, with just a few Arab fighters as guards. Bin Laden's method of travel varied, as well. Sometimes he journeyed by four-wheel-drive vehicle, while at other times he rode on horseback. Only a few of his trusted companions knew of his whereabouts at any given time.

Among these companions was a close friend of bin Laden's named Dr. Ayman al-Zawahiri, a medical doctor and former head of the ruthless terrorist group Egyptian Islamic Jihad. Al-Zawahiri was in charge of al-Qaeda's religious department, and he filled the role of father figure and spiritual guide that Abdullah Azzam had once occupied. In this role, al-Zawahiri exercised increasing influence over bin Laden's decision making and strategy. Al-Zawahiri also acted as bin Laden's personal physician. Since his return to Afghanistan, bin Laden had been experiencing problems with his health.

Dr. Ayman al-Zawahiri

Al-Zawahiri was born in 1951 to a rich and prominent Egyptian family. As a child, he was deeply religious. While he was at medical school in the 1960s, he became involved in radical Islamic groups. During the 1970s, while practicing as a pediatrician, he founded the terrorist group Egyptian Islamic Jihad. This group was responsible for the assassination of Egypt's president Anwar Sadat in 1981. Al-Zawahiri was angered by what he viewed as the corrupt elements in Egyptian society. His group was a sister organization to the Islamic Group, which burned down video stores, robbed jewelry shops, and killed tourists. Unlike the Islamic Group, al-Zawahiri's organization was highly secretive and concentrated its attacks on government targets.

In 1984 al-Zawahiri suddenly left Egypt to join the conflict in Afghanistan. He had been accused by several parents of molesting the children in his care, and his departure for Afghanistan may have been prompted by the beginning of a police investigation into these allegations. His family used their influence to suppress the investigation, and al-Zawahiri was never formally charged.

Al-Zawahiri first met bin Laden around 1985, and he was involved with al-Qaeda from the very beginning. The two men became very close during the period spent in Sudan, when al-Zawahiri was instrumental in several al-Qaeda operations.

He was troubled by low blood pressure, suffered frequent pains in his stomach and back, and was forced to walk with the aid of a cane. He also had a weak kidney, and he relied on a renal dialysis machine.

Al-Zawahiri, left, with Osama bin Laden, right. Al-Zawahiri radicalized bin Laden's views.

Like its founder, al-Qaeda had gone underground after the move to Afghanistan. The military wing of the organization was split up into small self-contained groupings, each largely ignorant of the activities of the other groups. This way, if an al-Qaeda operative were captured, he would not be able to divulge information about any activity beyond his own specific area. Only bin Laden, carefully keeping watch over al-Qaeda's different operations, knew that the group was gradually making progress toward a larger goal.

As his power and radicalism continued to grow, bin Laden made the war against the West more public by openly declaring a jihad on the United States.

Chapter **SIX**

JIHAD

BUOYED WITH CONFIDENCE AFTER SEVERAL successful operations, and knowing that the U.S. government would like to see him dead, bin Laden decided to make the conflict official. In August 1996, he issued his first *fatwa*, or religious ruling—a twelve-page document titled "The Declaration of War" that was written with the help of al-Zawahiri. It contained a warning to the United States to withdraw its military presence from Saudi Arabia, or else military action would be taken against it. A second fatwa was issued in February 1997 containing a similar message. Bin Laden, already a hero to many in the Arab world for standing up to the West, was becoming an object of interest to international media as well. He began to give interviews aired on TV networks such as CNN, ABC, and the BBC. For the first time, the general public in the United States and Europe became aware of the Saudi terrorist.

Despite having taken greater security precautions, two attempts were made on bin Laden's life in early 1997—both near misses. The first was a small bomb, placed close to a route into Jalalabad that bin Laden regularly followed. The second attack occurred in Jalalabad. Bin Laden was in the habit of visiting a former colleague from his days as a mujahideen, who was by then a senior officer in the Taliban's security service. Soon after bin Laden had left and driven away, a large bomb exploded, virtually destroying the nearby Jalalabad police station, killing 50 and injuring 150 people. It was not known who planted the bomb, but it had clearly been intended to kill bin Laden.

Bin Laden realized that Jalalabad was simply too dangerous a place for him to remain. Within weeks of the second attack, he and his family moved to Qandahar, in the heart of Taliban-controlled Afghanistan, where they occupied an old Soviet air force base close to the city's airport. For the time being, they were safe.

During this period, al-Zawahiri began to exercise increasing influence over bin Laden's strategy and public pronouncements. The Egyptian encouraged bin Laden to start including more references to the Palestinian struggle in his speeches. Al-Zawahiri encouraged bin Laden to tap into this well of bitterness to establish himself as a hero of the Palestinian cause.

Al-Zawahiri also shared bin Laden's radical view that al-Qaeda should widen its targets to include all Americans—even civilians. This policy was stated explicitly in a third fatwa issued by bin Laden in February 1998, which said, "The ruling to kill the Americans and their allies—civilians and military—is an individual duty for every Muslim who can do it in any country in which it is possible to do it, in order . . . for their armies to move out of all the lands of Islam, defeated and unable to threaten any Muslim."

Bin Laden backed up this threat with the announcement that same month of an anti-Western coalition called the World Islamic Front for Jihad Against Jews and Crusaders. Partners in this alliance included Sudan, Iraq, and Afghanistan, as well as various Arab and Asian terrorist and guerrilla groups. Bin Laden planned to use this newly assembled terrorist force to start launching major attacks against the United States and its allies.

TARGETING THE SNAKE

Although al-Zawahiri had persuaded bin Laden to adopt the Palestinian cause as his own, Palestine was not the most burning issue for the Saudi terrorist. The ongoing American presence in Saudi Arabia was, for bin Laden, the most urgent crisis for Islam. In an interview with ABC's *Nightline,* he told Americans, "You will leave

A rescue worker at the site of the bombed U.S. embassy in Nairobi, Kenya, in 1998

when the youth send you the wooden boxes and the coffins, and you will carry in it the bodies of American troops and civilians. This is when you will leave." Determined to make his intentions clear, bin Laden decided that it was time to take the fight directly to the United States, or to, as he described it, "cut off the head of the snake."

On August 7, 1998—the eighth anniversary of the arrival of American troops in Saudi Arabia in preparation for the Gulf War—a massive truck bomb demolished the U.S. embassy in Nairobi, Kenya, killing 213 people. Almost simultaneously, the U.S. embassy in Tanzania was also destroyed, killing 11.

The CIA soon found evidence linking al-Qaeda to the bombings. The United States retaliated by launching missile attacks at al-Qaeda training camps in Afghanistan and also at a pharmaceutical factory in Sudan suspected of manufacturing chemical weapons. However, these strikes only increased bin Laden's popularity in the Islamic world as the man who stood up to the well-armed U.S. forces.

It was quickly becoming clear that bin Laden was the number-one terrorist threat to the United States. However, the CIA was finding it difficult to trace his movements. They had the technical resources but lacked people with the language skills and cultural background to penetrate bin Laden's close-knit organization.

Bin Laden made the CIA's search harder by changing his location frequently. Every few days, a helicopter carried bin Laden hundreds of miles to a different part of the country, leaving his enemies with little chance of ever knowing where he was for long enough to plan an assassination. His refuges included the Hindu Kush and mountains located north of Qandahar. One of his favorite places was central Afghanistan, which was filled with inaccessible mountains and thousands of caves.

Surveillance of bin Laden by the CIA was also made problematic, if not impossible, by bin Laden's use of highly sophisticated communications equipment. He converted dozens of caves in the Afghan mountains into small command centers, with satellite fax and phone systems. These systems illegally tapped into foreign telephone networks, making them very difficult to trace. Bin Laden also stayed in touch with al-Qaeda cells around the world through the Internet, using encryption technology to disguise the messages.

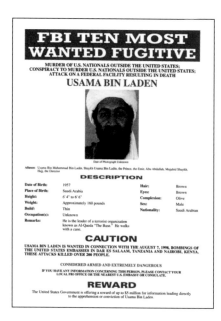

The FBI posted this notice on its website in 1999, as the U.S. government realized what a serious threat Osama bin Laden posed to the nation.

In November 1998, a federal grand jury in New York charged bin Laden with the murder of U.S. nationals in the August bombings of the U.S. embassies in Tanzania and Kenya. In June 1999, he was placed on the Federal Bureau of Investigation's (FBI) "Ten Most Wanted" list. A five-million-dollar reward was offered for information leading to his capture, the largest amount ever offered as a reward for a fugitive by the U.S. government.

On October 12, 2000, suicidal terrorists steered a bomb-laden boat to the port side of the American destroyer the USS *Cole* while it was docked in Yemen's Aden harbor. Seconds later, close to five hundred pounds of explosives detonated, blowing a hole forty

The damage inflicted by the bombing of the USS Cole, *shown above, was severe.*

feet in diameter in the ship's hull and killing seventeen American sailors. As usual, bin Laden denied any involvement, but the CIA soon discovered evidence linking al-Qaeda to the attack. Bin Laden did not refute this accusation. In fact, he added strength to these claims, without saying anything explicit, by releasing a videotape. Recorded before the attack, the video showed bin Laden and al-Zawahiri talking in vague terms about a future action but without mentioning the USS *Cole* by name. After the attack, bin Laden also made it clear that he was not concerned about U.S. retaliation. He released a statement to the *Jang*, a Pakistani newspaper, saying, "I am not afraid of American threats against me. As long as I am alive there will be no rest for the enemies of Islam. I will continue my mission against them."

WEAPONS OF MASS DESTRUCTION

Despite the success of al-Qaeda attacks on U.S. targets, bin Laden was frustrated by continued American presence on Saudi Arabian soil. He hoped that the recent terrorist strikes would express the anger of Islamic fundamentalists at the American government and that future attacks would gradually erode the United States' will to continue its policies in the Arab world. However, he realized that conventional methods would probably only achieve this goal over a very long period. To make a really decisive impact, he decided he would need weapons of mass destruction—that is, chemical, biological, or nuclear weapons—that could inflict death and devastation over a very wide area.

Chemical weapons contain substances such as nerve gas or poison, which can be released into the air or through air conditioning systems. Biological weapons are used to deliver biological agents, such as viruses and infectious diseases, into the air, through the water supply, or even through the postal system. Nuclear weapons have an explosive power that can devastate whole cities.

Evidence suggests that bin Laden was attempting to acquire weapons of mass destruction, both while he was in Sudan and later in Afghanistan. For example, there have been claims that bin Laden offered Chechen rebels a large amount of money to obtain for him an ex-Soviet nuclear device. Evidence of chemical weapons was found in soil tests from the site of the destroyed

Worries about al-Qaeda's access to chemical weapons were not new. In 1998 the United States had launched a missile attack on a Khartoum factory, above, suspected of producing a nerve agent that might then be provided for al-Qaeda's use.

pharmaceutical factory in Sudan. Satellite images showing fields in Afghanistan in which animals lay dead suggested that al-Qaeda had been testing biological weapons.

Bin Laden did not hide his ambitions to obtain such weapons. In an interview published in *Time* magazine he said, "Acquiring weapons for the defense of Muslims is a religious duty. If I have indeed acquired these weapons, I am carrying out a duty. It would be a sin for Muslims not to try to possess the weapons that would prevent the infidels from inflicting harm on Muslims."

AN EXPANDING FAMILY

In spite of his austere, security-conscious life, bin Laden continued to expand his immediate family, which had grown substantially since his marriage to his first wife. He had married again a few years later, this time to the cousin of Abu Sabaya, the head of an extremist Islamic group in the Philippines called Abu Sayyaf. Some time after his arrival in Afghanistan in 1996, bin Laden had strengthened his links with the Taliban leadership by marrying Fatima, the eldest daughter of Mullah Omar. Bin Laden took a fourth wife in 2000, marrying a Yemeni woman. This match strengthened relations with another group of Islamic militants, the al-Islah Party in northern Yemen. These marriages helped bin Laden secure alliances with important figures in the world of Islamic fundamentalism. They also allowed him to present the image of a powerful Arab sheikh.

From these four marriages, seventeen children were born. The family was too large and conspicuous to travel with bin Laden. His wives and children lived instead in various homes in and around the city of Qandahar, which bin Laden would occasionally visit. One rare family gathering took place in January 2001. The event was the wedding of bin Laden's son Mohammed to a daughter of al-Qaeda's military commander, Mohammed Atef, also known as Abu Hafs. A video of this event was made public, perhaps to convince the outside world that bin Laden was in good health, despite persistent rumors of illness. Another of bin Laden's sons, ten-year-old Hamza, wrote a poem for the occasion. Part of the poem read, "I am warning America that its people will face terrible consequences if they chase my father. Fighting Americans is the basis of faith." Bin Laden himself read the following poem, which many people believe is a reference to the bombing of the USS *Cole* the previous year:

> A destroyer: even the brave fear its might.
> It inspires horror in the harbor and in the open sea.
> She goes into the waves flanked by arrogance,
>   haughtiness and fake might.
> To her doom she progresses slowly, clothed in
>   a huge illusion.
> Awaiting her is a dinghy, bobbing in the waves.

Bin Laden's mother, Hamida, was one of the guests at Mohammed's wedding. Although bin Laden's relationship with her had been almost nonexistent when he was a child, it strengthened considerably in his adult years. After his exile from Saudi Arabia, he continued to speak to her regularly on the telephone, and she even visited him in Sudan in the early 1990s. After the Khobar Towers bombing, when the bin Ladens decided finally to have nothing more to do with him, Hamida was the only person from his former life with whom bin Laden stayed in touch—usually in brief calls on his satellite phone. She often pleaded with him to send his children back home so they could enjoy a more comfortable, settled life in Saudi Arabia, but bin Laden always refused. While the al-Sauds were in power, bin Laden would never send his family to Saudi Arabia.

U.S. troops entered Afghanistan in 2001 as a military response to the attacks of September 11.

Chapter SEVEN

THE WAR ON TERROR

ENCOURAGED BY AL-ZAWAHIRI, BIN LADEN increasingly saw the world as heading for an epic clash between the United States and its allies and the Islamic world—with himself and al-Qaeda at the front of the Islamic cause. The fight had already begun with al-Qaeda's attacks on U.S. interests abroad, including the 1993 World Trade Center attack, the 1996 Khobar Towers bombing in Saudi Arabia, the 1998 attacks on the U.S. embassies in Kenya and Tanzania, and the 2000 bombing of the USS *Cole*. But all of these strikes were a mere prelude to al-Qaeda's biggest attack yet—on the American homeland.

The attacks on the World Trade Center and the Pentagon on September 11, 2001, threw the United

President Bush visits Ground Zero—the site where the twin towers of the World Trade Center had once stood—three days after the attacks.

States and the world into a state of shock. They were the biggest and most ruthless terrorist attacks in history, claiming the lives of thousands of people. President George W. Bush helped to rally the nation's spirits with his defiant words, saying, "Terrorist attacks can shake the foundations of our biggest buildings, but they cannot touch the foundation of America. These acts shatter steel, but they cannot dent the steel of American resolve." After the September 11 attacks, the U.S. government declared a War on Terror and within weeks had assembled a coalition of nations to assist them in striking back against terrorists and their supporters.

Mounting evidence pointed to bin Laden as the culprit behind the attacks. Al-Qaeda also emerged as a suspect in the murder of the Northern Alliance leader Ahmad Shah Massoud. Massoud—whom many people had hoped might wrest power away from the Taliban and bring a more moderate government to Afghanistan— had been assassinated on September 9. Some observers speculated that al-Qaeda eliminated this potential rival to Taliban power so that he would not be able to take advantage of turmoil in Afghanistan after the

September 11 attacks. In addition, most of the hijackers who carried out the attacks were from Saudi Arabia, pointing to bin Laden's extensive network of loyal Arab Afghans and MAK veterans. All of the clues suggested that this had been a long-planned, highly orchestrated plot—and one that few groups other than al-Qaeda could have executed.

The bin Laden family responded to the attacks, and to the probability of Osama bin Laden's involvement, with shock and sadness. Abdullah Mohammed, a younger brother of bin Laden, said, "This is a tragedy for humanity. . . . This is a tragedy for our family." "All life is sacred," added Yeslam, another brother. "I condemn all killings and attacks against liberty and human values."

In the months following the September 11 attacks, bin Laden released several videotaped messages, many of which were broadcast on the Arabic-language satellite station al-Jazeera. These tapes were messages of defiance. In one, released on October 7, 2001, bin Laden declared that America would not live in peace until the Palestinians were restored to their homeland.

Meanwhile, the United States placed pressure on Afghanistan's Taliban leaders to hand over bin Laden. This was a dangerous time for the al-Qaeda leader. Although he had the unswerving loyalty of Mullah Omar, other factions within the Taliban leadership had grown less enamored of their guest. However, before any diplomatic efforts could potentially drive a wedge

Two police officers stand near a "Wanted" poster of Osama bin Laden in New York City.

between al-Qaeda and the Taliban, the military campaign by the United States and its allies began, and al-Qaeda and the Taliban joined forces to confront the international offensive.

Bin Laden appeared in public in November 2001 in the Islamic Studies Center in Jalalabad, where he addressed a group of about one thousand Afghan tribal leaders. He was dressed in gray robes and was surrounded by Arab fighters armed with rifles. According to witnesses, bin Laden said, "The Americans had a plan to invade, but if we are united and believe in

Allah we'll teach them a lesson, the same one we taught the Russians. God is with us, and we will win this war. Your Arab brothers will lead the way." After speaking, bin Laden departed in a two-hundred-vehicle convoy of al-Qaeda soldiers, heading for their mountain cave complex in the mountainous Tora Bora region of eastern Afghanistan.

Later that month, American B-52 jets repeatedly bombed the Tora Bora caves. Bin Laden was seen on November 26, after the bombing had started, by a group of his Yemeni fighters. He was reportedly drinking a glass of green tea and talking about the "holy war." According to U.S. and British intelligence, bin Laden survived the bombing and escaped to the Afghanistan-Pakistan border in early December. His Saudi cook claimed that he left on foot with an injured al-Qaeda operative, heading for Parachinar, just across the border.

Northern Alliance forces approached Kabul in November 2001, after the Taliban had fled the capital.

The Taliban continued to hold out in southern Afghanistan until December 2001, when they were overthrown by a combination of U.S.-led coalition forces waging war from the air and the U.S.-supported Northern Alliance on the ground. The Taliban was replaced by an interim government led by Hamid Karzai. Both the Taliban and al-Qaeda suffered heavy casualties, but bin Laden and Omar evaded capture. A full-scale hunt for them was launched, and the U.S. government offered twenty-five million dollars for information leading to bin Laden's capture or death.

On December 10, bin Laden's voice was heard on a shortwave radio transmission, encouraging his supporters to keep fighting. American forces had missed an opportunity to catch him at the border, leaving this task to Pakistani forces, who were not there in sufficient numbers to seal the long, mountainous border. A few days later, on December 13, a videotaped message was released in which bin Laden almost admitted involvement in the September 11 attacks, talking about how they had exceeded his own expectations. On December 22, a British man named Richard Reid attempted to blow up a transatlantic flight to the United States by igniting explosives packed in his shoes. Known afterward as the "shoe bomber," Reid was believed to have links to al-Qaeda and bin Laden. However, bin Laden himself was still nowhere to be found. For the time being, he had disappeared from view.

WHAT NEXT FOR AL-QAEDA?

Al-Qaeda is not an organization that is likely to compromise. Bin Laden has established a mindset within the group's membership to ensure that they will fight to the death. Although bin Laden's and top aide al-Zawahiri's whereabouts are unknown, al-Qaeda is not likely to deviate from the course that these two have set.

However, bin Laden and al-Zawahiri have not always agreed on every aspect of al-Qaeda's future. Al-Zawahiri, in view of Afghanistan's continuing instability, wishes to move the organization to a safer location so that it can rebuild to fight another day. Bin Laden, the former mujahideen, has sworn to fight to the death in Afghanistan against the U.S.-backed government. So far, bin Laden's view has prevailed, and al-Qaeda's forces, having merged with the ousted Taliban, have positioned themselves along the Afghanistan-Pakistan border, from where they are preparing to wage a guerrilla campaign that may last for years.

Experts expect al-Qaeda to continue to coordinate its global network, although it will have to keep finding new ways of communicating and moving people and money around to evade increasingly watchful governments. As part of the ongoing War on Terror waged by the United States and other governments, al-Qaeda training camps in Afghanistan have been bombed. Suspected terrorist cells around the world have been investigated, and terrorist assets have been frozen. Nevertheless, al-Qaeda cells remain intact in many parts of the world. Many members have been captured and killed, but recruitment of new members is never a problem. Many young Muslims who face poverty and other hardships see al-Qaeda and similar radical groups as outlets for their despair and anger.

To many, bin Laden remains an icon and a symbol of resistance to the enemies of Islam. Bin Laden has been more successful than other Islamic leaders in attracting Muslims to his cause because he is willing to cut across the boundaries that divide many Muslims, such as the division between the Sunni and Shiite branches of the faith. He tries to bridge differences of geography and belief and to unite Islam into one force.

Bin Laden appeals to devout Muslims because he always presents himself as a man of God—despite his lack of formal religious training—by peppering his speeches with quotes from the Quran and suggesting that his actions are guided by Allah. He tries to appear as a man of peace, forced into aggressive acts in response to the killing of Muslims and the violation of Islamic holy sites by Western nations. His frequent references to the Palestinian struggle have endeared him to many people in that movement.

Perhaps most significantly to thousands of his admirers, bin Laden has been uncompromising and fearless in his attitude toward the United States. He has never wavered in his anti-American stance, and this resolute hostility has won him support in many parts of

Demonstrators in Karachi, Pakistan, declare their support for Osama bin Laden.

Muslim Asia and Africa. "Long Live bin Laden" posters were in evidence at anti-United States demonstrations in Malaysia and Indonesia toward the end of 2001. Since September 11, thousands of children born to Muslim parents around the world have been named Osama bin Laden.

Many people believe that it is only a matter of time before bin Laden, as the world's most wanted man, is killed or captured. In the meantime, there are plenty of rumors about his whereabouts. Some believe he is in Chechnya. According to others, he is in southeastern

Afghanistan, or maybe in the Pakistani border town of Mirim Shah. Various videotapes featuring bin Laden surfaced in the months after his disappearance, one of which showed him and al-Zawahiri gloating over the success of the September 11 attacks. The backgrounds of these videos were painstakingly analyzed for clues about when and where they were shot, but nothing conclusive could be drawn from them.

According to sources in Saudi Arabia, bin Laden's mother received a handwritten note from him at the beginning of March 2002. The letter said, "I am in good health, and I am in a very, very safe place. They will never get me, unless God wills it." The letter concluded, "You will hear good news very soon." Bin Laden may have been referring to the "dirty bomb" attack planned by al-Qaeda operative Jose Padilla. A dirty bomb has nuclear material packed around it. When it explodes, radioactive fallout can spread over a large area and buildings can be contaminated. In addition, the fear of radioactivity can cause widespread panic. In May 2002, Padilla was arrested by FBI agents at Chicago's O'Hare Airport, after he had flown in from Pakistan. He was accused of planning to bomb a U.S. city.

Meanwhile, a new sighting of bin Laden was reported. An al-Qaeda commander hiding in Pakistan told an Arabic-language newspaper that bin Laden had been wounded at Tora Bora but was recovering. The next clue to bin Laden's whereabouts came in November 2002, when al-Jazeera played an audio recording of a man who claimed to be bin Laden. The man boasted of recent terrorist attacks, including a devastating bombing of nightclubs in Bali. He also warned Western governments that aggression toward Arab nations would only result in more attacks. Analysis of the tape led Western intelligence agencies to confirm that the recording was indeed bin Laden's voice. That same month, attacks on an Israeli airliner and an Israeli-owned hotel in Mombasa, Kenya, were also believed to be the work of bin Laden's organization. And, although high-ranking al-Qaeda members including chief of operations Khalid Sheikh Mohammed and lieutenant Tawfiq Attash Khallad were captured that year, the group remained active. In May 2003, suicide bombers believed to be working for al-Qaeda struck sites in Saudi Arabia and Morocco in attacks aimed at Westerners.

But bin Laden himself remains elusive. If he is alive, he may be with al-Zawahiri. His son Abdullah and a few top members of al-Qaeda could also be with him, protected by an elite guard of fighters. He could be moving among camouflaged bunkers dotted around Afghanistan or the Afghanistan-Pakistan border, rarely staying anywhere for more than one night.

Whatever his fate, bin Laden's legacy is assured and the verdict on his life already pronounced. To a minority of people who rejoice in violence against the West, he will remain a hero. To most other people, he is a villain whose twisted vision of Islam has destroyed the lives of thousands and wrought disaster on the world.

SOURCES

11   Cable News Network, "September 11: Chronology of Terror,"
      CNN.com/U.S., September 12, 2001,
      <http://www.cnn.com/2001/US/09/11/chronology.attack/>
      (November 28, 2002).

21   Adam Robinson, *Bin Laden: Behind the Mask of the Terrorists*
      (New York: Arcade Publishing, 2002), 52.

24   Ibid., 54.

26–27 Jason Burke, "The Making of Osama bin Laden," *Salon.com*,
      November 1, 2001,
      <http://archive.salon.com/news/feature/2001/11/01/osama_profile>
      (November 15, 2002).

27   Ibid.

30   Ibid.

35   Peter L. Bergen, *Holy War, Inc.: Inside the Secret World of
      Osama bin Laden* (London: Weidenfeld & Nicholson, 2001), 57.

37–38 Paul Watson, Tyler Marshall, and Bob Drogin, "The Deadly
      Disciple of Terror: Bin Laden's Privileged Birth Gave Way to
      Life of Hatred," *News Journal*, September 16, 2001,
      <http://www.delawareonline.com/newsjournal/local/2001/09/
      16thedeadlydiscip.html> (November 15, 2002).

42   Rohan Gunaratna, *Inside al-Qaeda: Global Network of Terror*
      (New York: Columbia University Press, 2002), 20.

44–45 Burke, "The Making of Osama bin Laden."

45   Bergen, *Holy War, Inc.*, 134.

47   Burke, "The Making of Osama bin Laden."

54–55 John Miller, "To Terror's Source," *ABC News*, 1998,
      <http://more.abcnews.go.com/sections/world/DailyNews/
      miller_binladen_980609.html> (November 15, 2002).

57   Peter Bergen, "An Elusive Warlord's Deadly 'Sleepers'," *Fox News
      Channel*, September 17, 2001, <http://www.foxnews.com/story/
      0,2933,34441,00.html> (November 28, 2002).

64   Bergen, *Holy War, Inc.*, 86–87.

64–65 Alan Feuer, "Bin Laden Group Had Extensive Network of
      Companies, Witness Says," *New York Times*, February 13, 2001.

67   Miller, "To Terror's Source."

67–68 Gunaratna, *Inside al-Qaeda*, 35.

68   Bergen, *Holy War, Inc.*, 97.

72–73 Ibid., 102.

76   Robinson, *Bin Laden: Behind the Mask of the Terrorists*, 200.

85   Gunaratna, *Inside al-Qaeda*, 46.

85–86   Miller, "To Terror's Source."

89   "Terrorist to US: Don't Retaliate," *CBS News*, October 17, 2001, <http://www.cbsnews.com/stories/2000/10/17/world/main241791.shtml> (November 15, 2002).

91   Gunaratna, *Inside al-Qaeda*, 48.

92–93   Robinson, *Bin Laden: Behind the Mask of the Terrorists*, 271.

93   Reuters, "To Her Doom," *abcNEWS.com*, March 1, 2001, <http://abcnews.go.com/sections/world/DailyNews/afghanistan010301_binladen.html> (November 28, 2002).

96   "Bush Addresses Nation: Full Text," *BBC News*, September 12, 2001, <http://news.bbc.co.uk/1/hi/world/americas/1539328.stm> (November 15, 2002).

97   Robinson, *Bin Laden: Behind the Mask of the Terrorists*, 11.

97   Ibid.

98–99   Jane Corbin, "The Great Escape: Where Is Osama bin Laden?" *Sunday Times*, June 30, 2002.

104   Ibid.

SELECTED BIBLIOGRAPHY

Bergen, Peter L. *Holy War, Inc.: Inside the Secret World of Osama bin Laden*. London: Weidenfeld & Nicholson, 2001.

"Bin Laden, Millionaire with a Dangerous Grudge." *CNN*. September 27, 2001. <http://www.cnn.com/2001/US/09/12/binladen.profile> (November 15, 2002).

Burke, Jason. "The Making of Osama bin Laden." *Salon.com* November 1, 2001. <http://dir.salon.com/news/feature/2001/11/01/osama_profile> (November 15, 2002).

"Bush Addresses Nation: Full Text." *BBC News*. September 12, 2001. <http://news.bbc.co.uk/1/hi/world/americas/1539328.stm> (November 15, 2002).

Corbin, Jane. "The Great Escape: Where Is Osama bin Laden?" *Sunday Times*, June 30, 2002.

Feuer, Alan. "Bin Laden Group Had Extensive Network of Companies, Witness Says." *New York Times*, February 13, 2001.

Gunaratna, Rohan. *Inside al-Qaeda: Global Network of Terror*. New York: Columbia University Press, 2002.

Miller, John. "Greetings, America. My Name Is Osama bin Laden." *Esquire*, February 1999.

———. "To Terror's Source," *ABC News*. 1998. <http://more.abcnews.go.com/sections/world/DailyNews/miller_binladen_980609.html> (November 15, 2002).

"Osama bin Laden: Suspected Terrorist Mastermind." *ABC News*. N.d. <http://abcnews.go.com/sections/world/DailyNews/binladen_newsmakerbio.html> (November 15, 2002).

Robinson, Adam. *Bin Laden: Behind the Mask of the Terrorists*. New York: Arcade Publishing, 2002.

"Terrorist to US: Don't Retaliate." *CBS News*. October 17, 2001. <http://www.cbsnews.com/stories/2000/10/17/world/main241791.shtml> (July 2002).

Watson, Paul, Tyler Marshall, and Bob Drogin. "The Deadly Disciple of Terror: Bin Laden's Privileged Birth Gave Way to Life of Hatred." *News Journal*, September 16, 2001. <http://www.delawareonline.com/newsjournal/local/2001/09/16thedeadlydiscip.html> (November 15, 2002).

"Who Is Osama bin Laden?" *BBC News*. September 18, 2001. <http://news.bbc.co.uk/1/hi/world/south_asia/155236.stm> (November 15, 2002).

"Who Is Osama bin Laden and What Does He Want?" *PBS*. N.d. <http://www.pbs.org/wgbh/pages/frontline/shows/binladen/who> (November 15, 2002).

FOR FURTHER READING

Behnke, Alison. *Afghanistan in Pictures*. Minneapolis: Lerner Publications Company, 2003.

Broberg, Catherine. *Saudi Arabia in Pictures*. Minneapolis: Lerner Publications Company, 2003.

Currie, Stephen. *Terrorists and Terrorist Groups*. San Diego: Lucent Books, 2002.

Katz, Samuel M. *Jerusalem or Death: Palestinian Terrorism*. Minneapolis: Lerner Publications Company, 2004.

———. *Jihad: Islamic Fundamentalist Terrorism*. Minneapolis: Lerner Publications Company, 2004.

Moktefi, Mokhtar. *The Arabs in the Golden Age*. Translated by Mary Kae LaRose. Brookfield, CT: Millbrook Press, 1992.

Santella, Andrew. *September 11, 2001*. New York: Children's Press, 2002.

Sherrow, Victoria. *The World Trade Center Bombing: Terror in the Towers*. Springfield, NJ: Enslow, 1998.

Spencer, William. *Islamic Fundamentalism in the Modern World*. Brookfield, CT: Millbrook Press, 1995.

Taus-Bolstad, Stacy. *Pakistan in Pictures*. Minneapolis: Lerner Publications Company, 2003.

Taylor, Robert. *History of Terrorism*. San Diego: Lucent Books, 2002.

INDEX

OTHER TITLES FROM LERNER AND A&E®:

Arthur Ashe
The Beatles
Benjamin Franklin
Bill Gates
Bruce Lee
Carl Sagan
Chief Crazy Horse
Christopher Reeve
Colin Powell
Daring Pirate Women
Edgar Allan Poe
Eleanor Roosevelt
George W. Bush
George Lucas
Gloria Estefan
Jack London
Jacques Cousteau
Jane Austen
Jesse Owens
Jesse Ventura
Jimi Hendrix
John Glenn
Latin Sensations
Legends of Dracula

Legends of Santa Claus
Louisa May Alcott
Madeleine Albright
Malcolm X
Mark Twain
Maya Angelou
Mohandas Gandhi
Mother Teresa
Nelson Mandela
Oprah Winfrey
Princess Diana
Queen Cleopatra
Queen Elizabeth I
Queen Latifah
Rosie O'Donnell
Saddam Hussein
Saint Joan of Arc
Thurgood Marshall
Tiger Woods
William Shakespeare
Wilma Rudolph
Women in Space
Women of the Wild West
Yasser Arafat

ABOUT THE AUTHOR

Alex Woolf studied history and government at Essex University and earned an advanced diploma in publishing studies at Oxford Brookes University, both in the United Kingdom. He has worked as an editor for more than ten years, developing many history and social studies series for children. In 2001 he became a freelance writer, specializing in twentieth-century history and politics.

PHOTO ACKNOWLEDGMENTS

Images used with the permission of: © Popperfoto/Reuters, pp. 2, 13 (Eric Draper/The White House/HO), 46 (Dominique Dudouble), 48, 61, 75 (Dylan Martinez), 76, 77, 86 (Corinne Dufka), 88, 94 (POOL/ Joe), 96, 98; © Rex Features, pp. 6, 10 (Tamara Beckwith), 89; © Popperfoto, pp. 14, 28, 29, 56, 63, 69, 70 (Patrick de Noirmont), 99 (Yannis Behrakis); © Camera Press, pp. 17, 26; © Topham Picturepoint, pp. 19, 20 (ImageWorks), 34, 38, 40 (AP), 54 (John Moore/ImageWorks), 57 (Photri), 103 (Ilyas Dean/ ImageWorks); © Corbis, pp. 23 (Charles & Josette Lenars), 91 (Attar Maher/ SYGMA); © Rex Features/Sipa Press, pp. 32, 42, 66, 81, 82.

Cover photos (hardcover and paperback): front and back © AFP/Corbis

WEBSITES

Website addresses in this book were valid at the time of printing. However, because of the nature of the Internet, some addresses may have changed or sites may have closed since publication. While the author, packager, and Publisher regret any inconvenience this may cause readers, no responsibility for any such changes can be accepted by the author, packager, or Publisher.